A Business Guide
for Beginners

A Business Guide for Beginners

An explanation of business concepts and terminology

Des O'Keeffe

Legend ⬛ Business

Independent Book Publisher

Legend Business, 2 London Wall Buildings,
London EC2M 5UU
business@legend-paperbooks.co.uk
www.legendpress.co.uk

Contents © Des O'Keeffe 2010

British Library Cataloguing in Publication Data available.

ISBN 978-1-9074611-8-7

Set in Times
Printed by Lightning Source, Milton Keynes.

Cover designed by EA Digital, Leicester
www.eadigital.com

Independent Book Publisher

Acknowledgements

I'd like to express my thanks to Tom Chalmers and Jonathan Reuvid for supporting me with this venture, and to Jonathan for his helpful suggestions regarding the text. I'd also like to thank Allan Gray and Jonathan English for their advice and encouraging comments, Marina Hodder for her assistance with preparing the manuscript, and finally to the many students who kept on motivating me to take on this challenge.

Author

Des O'Keeffe has a BA in Classics from the University of Durham and an MBA from the University of Bradford. During a 30-year financial career he worked in a variety of well-known companies in the UK before moving to Central Europe with the Calor Group. He helped set up Tesco's Hungarian operation as their Financial Director. He also undertook a financial directorship, within a large telecommunications group, in Poland. Des has been teaching since 2003. He teaches business English at a major language school in Portsmouth and has also taught finance on the MBA course at the Technical University in Riga, Latvia.

Contents

A Few Words to Start

This is not a difficult book. However, not all the material is simple. I have a strong belief that complex or difficult subjects can be easily understood if explained simply, which is why I became a teacher. I once spent half a winter struggling through a weekly two and a half hour finance evening class, becoming tired, irritated, stressed and confused, before attending a crash revision course given by my employers at which many of the "difficult " concepts were explained in a matter of minutes.

I have two objectives in writing this book: first, to help you if you are considering going into the business world, or starting a course of business study, but you feel fear because you are not confident in your understanding of business concepts or terminology. Second, if you decide to give business a go, to give you some ideas, and hopefully motivation, for approaching your venture into the business world. I've referred to people as "he" for simplicity but this of course is "gender blind".

I've kept to the traditional business areas. I've not gone into the area of leading edge, or virtual technology, as these are specialist areas and subject to constant development, nor the area of e-commerce, as I think most people understand the terminology through day to day usage. Nor have I tried to make any predictions about the future of business.

I don't claim to possess all knowledge – business is complex. I have, however, "been around a bit", in organisations large and small, traditional and state of the art, in the UK and overseas, working at the bottom and nearer the top, in the public and private sectors. I started my business life as the lift operator in a textile company (where the lift was summoned by banging on the wall) and have had director status of what is now one of Europe's top 30 companies. I'm confident that the book will give you a summary picture of the main business concepts which is accurate enough to be of enormous help.

Part 1

Introduction to Business

Let's start at the beginning.

? *What is business?*

Business is something serious which occupies us. To be busy is to be occupied. If I'm "going about my business", I'm occupied with the important things of my life. Business is something which concerns us all. In fact, another name for a business organisation is a **concern**. If we say "it's none of your business" or "it's not your concern" we are saying the same thing.

When we talk about business as a study topic, however, we need to go a bit further. If I occupy myself in the serious task of painting your house, but make no charge, this is not business. I'm only doing business when I'm doing it for a profit or to make a livelihood.

All business involves **goods** and **services**. We **supply** goods and **provide** services to **customers**. In order to do business, when we are the customer we **source** goods from **suppliers** and **receive** services from **providers**.

So the language of the basic business model is like this:

Figure 1.1 Language of the basic business model

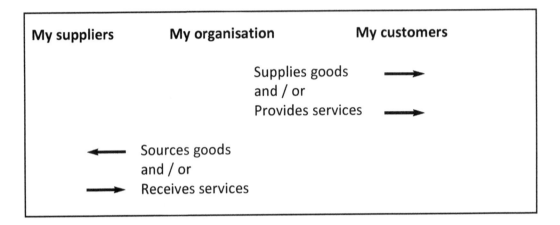

The goods and services must be what the customer wants. If the customer does not want, or has not asked for, what he receives, then he is being cheated. This is called a **scam**. If the customer is forced to pay for something which he do not need, this is **extortion**.

We can define business, therefore, like this:

The provision of goods and services in satisfaction of customer requirements in order to make a gain

Here, "**provision**", to make the definition short, refers to both supplying goods and providing services.

The objective of a business must be for the organisations to increase in wealth. This would normally mean making a **profit**, that is a financial gain, but not always. For example, business may not involve money but may simply involve the exchange of goods. If I exchange sheep for wine with the intention of becoming more wealthy (known as "**barter**") then I am conducting business.

Business and the Economy

The UK economy consists of the **private and the public sectors**. In such a "**mixed economy**", the private and public sectors join to form a "**free market economy**".

Figure 1.2 Composition of the total economy

PUBLIC SECTOR + PRIVATE SECTOR	= TOTAL ECONOMY = MIXED ECONOMY = FREE MARKET ECONOMY

Both the public and private sectors contain business and non-business organisations.

Non-profit organisations

Some private or public sector non-business organisations are categorised as "not–for-profit", (or "non-profit") organisations, but it's a difficult area and not all non-business organisations are called "not-for-profit". A non-profit organisation (NPO) could best be described as an organisation that has income but does not distribute its surplus money to its owners or shareholders. Instead it uses it to help pursue its goals. Examples of NPOs include charitable organisations, trade unions, and public arts organisations". (1)

It's simpler to talk about "business" and "non-business".

The business activity of the economy forms a free market in which consumers can choose from a variety of products or services offered for sale by competitive suppliers. These may be public or private sector suppliers.

The **private sector** is, of course, privately owned, and is managed by private individuals or organisations, not by the state (the government).

The **public sector** is owned and managed by the state on behalf of the people (the **public**). Ownership of organisations by the government in the public sector may be total or on a majority basis. Operations in the public sector are also financed by the state and therefore, ultimately, by the public through taxation.

In the UK and the US private sector, business is much more prevalent than public sector business. There is relatively little business operating commercially (i.e. generating revenue) in the public sector in the UK. Public sector commercial business includes a small proportion of transport, the Post Office, and energy and utility (for example water) companies.

Profit and the public sector

A public sector organisation may or may not exist in order to make a profit.

Over the last fifty years UK public sector organisations have been increasingly run on commercial lines – in other words they have been driven more towards the financial result and less towards simply providing an essential service irrespective of the financial result. However, in addition to owning and running public sector organisations, the government also still exercises an influence over them. Because of this, activities in the public sector are not confined to the optimisation of the financial result but are still also influenced by social interest. A public sector hospital, which does not aim to make a profit, and the Post Office, which does, both have as their objectives provision of the best possible service for the public and must balance this with operating in the most economically advantageous way for the public.

? *What does the UK public sector consist of?*

The UK public sector includes:

- health and education
- tax, customs, excise
- government (central and local)
- the emergency services

- the armed forces
- the Post Office
- some transport
- broadcasting (the BBC)
- the judiciary

The question then is:

If an organisation does not make a profit, is it still a business?

The Post Office is clearly a business as it is (especially at the moment) being hard-driven to maximise profit. It attempts to compete with private sector companies in the areas of banking and parcel delivery, despite having to meet the requirements of providing an excellent service for society at large.

What, however, about a non-profit making organisation like a hospital? Here the organisation is not financed from sales revenue but from a charge on the public. However, the concept of "customer" still applies. A public sector hospital attempts to provide the best possible service for its customers at the optimum cost. The customers are those who use it – patients and dependants of patients – and those who pay for it. These latter are: immediately, central and local government and, ultimately, the general public. Although several factors normally associated with "business" – **service, customer,** and **optimal financial result** – are present in the running of a state hospital, the organisation cannot be labelled "a business" because its ultimate objective is not to make profit.

Command economy
An economy which consists only of a public sector, i.e. where the state attempts to control all commercial activity, and where any private business by individuals or organisations is restricted to illegal or unofficial transactions, is called a **command economy**.

A command economy is the opposite of a free market economy. In a command economy the state decides what to make available:

1.3 How a command economy functions

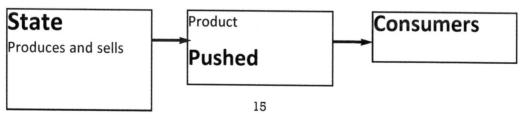

State
Produces and sells

Product
Pushed

Consumers

I experienced a command economy in 1983 when I visited Prague, capital of what was then Czechoslovakia. The country had been Communist since 1946. There appeared to be no private advertising whatsoever. A drinks bar was indicated by a hole in a wall on the other side of which people were drinking. There was no sign, and no lights to mark it. There appeared to be two products on sale: "beer" and "sandwich". Units of consumption were recorded by a pencil mark on a piece of cardboard. This was my introduction to a command economy, where the state decides what is produced and sold and the consumers have no choice: they either buy and consume what is available or have nothing.

Private sector business

Let's focus on the private sector. The private sector consists of business and non-business.

The main types of private sector organisation are:

Business	Non-Business
sole trader	charities
partnership	private schools
limited companies	foundations
private hospitals	clubs, societies, religious organisations etc.

The distinction between business and non-business can become a little difficult. As we've seen, one question is: does the organisation distribute its surplus funds to owners or shareholders? I would say that a private hospital, whilst aiming to provide an excellent service for patients, exists to make a profit, does distribute its surplus funds to its owners, and therefore is a business. A private school, whilst it may generate wealth from its **feepayers**, does not distribute its surplus funds to its owners, and therefore is not a business.

Business organisations in a the private sector of a free market economy focus on satisfying the needs of the market. They operate something like Figure 1.4:

Figure 1.4 How private sector organisations function

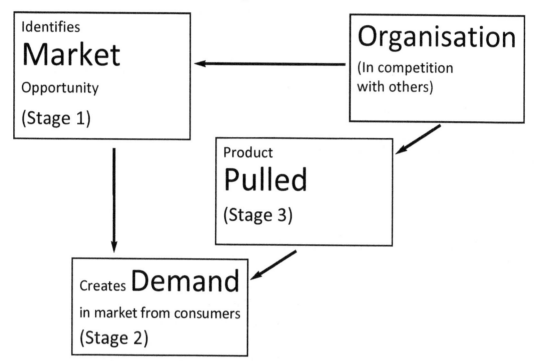

A **sole trader** is a business organisation, owned and managed by one person, e.g. an electrician or a consultant. "Trading" is literally about buying and selling but the term "sole trader" can be used of anybody providing services.

A **partnership** is an organisation owned and managed by a group of people who are also responsible for running the business, for example, a firm of lawyers or doctors. The partners share the profit but, unless some specific protection is arranged, the owners will be responsible to pay for losses or financial damage caused to others.

 So, what's a limited company?

A **limited company** is a business organisation owned by **shareholders** (who hold **shares**) and run by **directors**. The shares have a **nominal value**, which stays the same, and a **market value**, which goes up and down according to how good an investment the shares are judged to be by the market. The shareholders hope to gain financially in two ways:

- As the company prospers, the market value of the shares will normally go up, so the investor can make a profit if he then sells his shares (a **"capital gain"**).

- Part of the profit which the company makes can be distributed to the shareholders in the form of **"dividend"**. This is referred to as **"income"** to the shareholder.

(?) What does "limited" mean?

Companies are referred to as "limited" because the liability of the owners is limited or restricted.

(?) What does "liability" mean?

"Liability" means legal financial responsibility. Liability of the owners of an organisation means the legal responsibility to pay for losses or financial damage caused by the organisation to others. "Limited liability" in respect of company shareholders means that any responsibility to pay is restricted to the issue price payable for the shares they hold. Of course, if the company makes a loss, or runs into financial difficulty, dividend payments to the shareholders are also likely to be stopped.
So:

a limited company is a commercial organisation, owned by shareholders, where any liability of the individual owners is limited to the amount payable for the shares they hold

A limited company may be public or private. *This has nothing to do with the public sector: almost all limited companies are in the private sector.*

(?) What's a PLC?

According to the Wikipedia definition, "a **public limited company** (PLC) .....is a type of limited liability company in the United Kingdom and the Republic of Ireland... which is permitted to offer its shares to the public. It may be listed on a stock exchange to be publicly traded." (2)

It is, actually, possible for a the shares in a PLC to be wholly owned by the government.

A private company (sorry, it's not referred to as a PLC even though it is a private limited company) is a company where the shares are not listed on a stock exchange, and are not publicly traded, but are privately held.

What is the structure of a limited company?

A British PLC is run, not by the shareholders, but on behalf of the shareholders by the directors. Collectively the directors are called the **"Board"** and the head of the board is the **Chairman**. The terms **"President"** and **"Vice President"** are not used in UK legally registered companies. Each director has legal responsibilities in respect of running the business.

The chairman does not normally run the company but has more of a "figure-head" role. He is responsible for representing the company, especially to the shareholders and to the financial institutions who may lend to or invest in the com-pany. The senior director involved in the day to day running of the company is the **Managing Director**, but he may also be called the **CEO** (Chief Executive Officer).

Figure 1.5 The typical hierarchy of a UK PLC

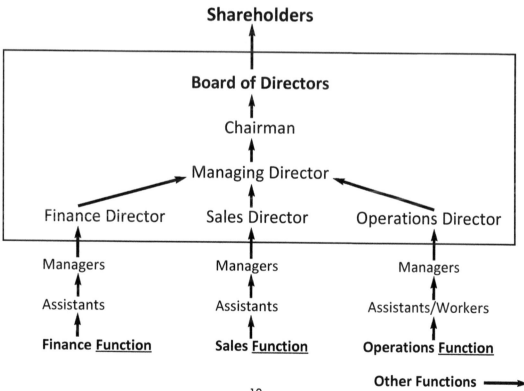

The different areas of which the company consists (finance, sales, technical, etc.) are called **"functions"** and, generally, are each headed up by a director.

So, the typical UK PLC hierarchy looks like Figure 1.5 above.

The chairman and directors may be **executive** or **non-executive**. An executive chairman or director performs a full-time role in the company. A non-executive director does not have a full-time role but attends meetings and contributes to the decision making of the board.

The word **"staff"**, has two meanings: it describes somebody who works for somebody ("he has two staff/management and staff"). It also refers to employees who work in offices – staff are sometimes referred to as **"white collar"**. Employees who work in production are called **"workers"**, sometimes called **"blue collar"**. Everybody in the organisation, **employers** and **employees,** are the **workforce**. (The **labour force** are the people available to work from the surrounding geographical area).

Some Key Success Concepts

As we take a tour around the world of business I'll try to highlight a few key success themes. Business organisations can tip very quickly from success to failure: at the end of 2000, the Enron Corporation had a market value of $70bn. By the end of 2001, it was in bankruptcy. In 2006, Lehman Bros, the financial services giant employing over 26,000 people, reported an increase in net profit of 23% to $4bn. In 2008 they filed for bankruptcy; such a shockwave resulted that financial markets were destabilised worldwide.

One view of corporate success is that if a company exists to make a profit for its shareholders, then the only determiner of success is how much profit it makes. An alternative view is that a company must balance its profit objective with the requirement to operate not only in a legal way but also an **ethical** way.

How can a business keep on maximising its profit?

Successful companies have a concept of **excellence**: they strive to be excellent in everything they do. They have excellent products and services, and often, also, have an excellent approach to **business ethics** and **corporate governance** (I'll explain this later).

Here are some of the specific things which are vital to excellence, and therefore to success:

Market
The "West" consists of free market economies. Successful companies give high priority to marketing. This is not only about advertising: it means that they

understand the market in which they are operating, including the actions of competitors. They watch the market closely and monitor any changes. They offer a product which the market wants, and they do everything they can to make the market want to buy it. In business, the market rules.

When I was discussing the possibility of this book, the first questions were: "Is there a market for this type of book?" and "Are there any competing books on the market?"

Quality
Successful companies achieve excellence through having great products – which can include services. Quality is a key interface between the company and its customers. Successful companies have excellent products and service. They have user-friendly systems and excellent quality standards. This does not mean they aim for perfection in all aspects of quality. It means they set appropriate standards and try to achieve them.

People
Excellent companies aim at attracting, recruiting, and keeping the best people. They understand the importance of people in an organisation. They get things done by getting the best out of individuals and teams by **empowerment**. Excellent companies pay attention to the needs of their people and are rewarded with energy and great performance. As a result, excellent companies do not employ demotivated people, or people working below par. Excellent companies are fun to work in.

Focus
Excellent companies focus on the key drivers of their business. They have clear strategies and objectives which are agreed at the top level and which "cascade" down the organisation through clear information channels. They constantly generate ideas and try new things, but they don't change products, markets or policies without careful consideration and communication. They don't take unnecessary risks. They "plan the work and work the plan". In excellent companies "all the heads point in the same direction", and, in excellent companies, that normally means towards the market.

Simplicity
Americans have an acronym **"KISS"** which means:

KEEP IT **SIMPLE**, STUPID!!

There's a connection between success and simplicity. Successful companies prefer simple structures and like to split the organisation into manageable and understandable units. Simplicity, in procedures and systems, is key to service. Simplicity is also a key to personal success. People won't respond to you, speak well of you or promote you if they don't understand you.

Part 2

The Main Functional Areas of a Company

The actual division of a company into "functions" varies from company to company; however, the functions which are detailed below, whilst not covering every one, are common to most companies.

- People Management
- Marketing
- Finance
- Operations
- Quality

Let's consider them one by one.

People Management

Here's a key question:

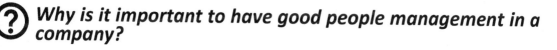 ***Why is it important to have good people management in a company?***

Good people management normally leads to happy and motivated people.

Why is it important for a company to have happy people?

Happy people:

- are motivated, so they work harder and better, and therefore produce more, and produce at a higher quality;

- cause fewer problems;

- stay in the company longer, thereby reducing the enormous cost of loss of experience and of recruitment and training of new people;

- represent the company better, for example in the area of customer service;

- generate more ideas for improvement;

- generate an energised work culture, which in turn leads to happy and motivated people.

So what makes people happy and motivated in an organisation?

Countless books have been written on the subject of motivation. Sandra Dawson, Professor of Management and Deputy Vice Chancellor of the University of Oxford, points to the following three major factors: (3)

- financial packages;

- good tools for the job (for example, management information and manu-facturing systems);

- the opportunity for advancement and development in the organisation.

I also think that for most people it's extremely important to be able to *contribute*. The majority of people, in my experience, are not at all lazy, but need some understanding of what their boss is trying to do. Normally the whole organisation is too big to relate to: people like working for people, not mission statements. If a boss can communicate his desires and objectives to his people, and his people have an opportunity to contribute, they will be normally be happy.

So what does give an organisation good people management?

The following things lead to good people management in an organisation:

- Top level buy-in. An organisation's people management strategy is not likely to work unless it is supported and driven by the people at the top, and this strategy "cascades" down the organisation.

- A suitable organisation structure. People are not likely to perform well if there are too many levels, too many bosses, or too many people to bump into as they try to do their job.

- An effective Human Resources department. **Human Resources (HR),** sometimes called **Personnel** in smaller companies, is the function in a company responsible for organisational aspects of people management.

- Great managers. This is probably the most important factor. It is vital that people like (or at least do not dislike) their boss, are clear as to what they should do, and are not being prevented from doing it.

OK, so what does HR do?

HR is responsible for putting in place, and maintaining, the things which allow effective people management in an organisation. The key responsibilities of HR are as follows:

- **Training.**

- **Staff appraisal.** This is a formally documented process, performed by managers on their people, which aims to communicate to them how they are performing, and to discuss what they need in order to improve and develop.

- **Staff development.** This refers to all the processes in the company designed to identify the people with potential, keep them in the organisation, and prepare them for, and get them into, the right positions.

- **Arbitration** and management of **disputes**. Disputes may be between the organisation on the one hand and either an individual or staff negotiating together on the other. If an individual thinks that the organisation is treating him unfairly, this is known as a **grievance**. If people try to negotiate together, usually through **trade unions**, who represent them, this is known as **collective bargaining** and the process as a whole, which involves HR is called **industrial relations.**

- **Discipline and dismissal.** HR has the responsibility to recommend the correct action in cases where employees do something unlawful at work or contravene company policies and procedures. The usual formal procedure is one or two warnings followed by **dismissal**. Dismissal relates to situations where there is a problem with the employee or his work. (**Redundancy** relates to the situation where there is no work for the employee).

- **Policies and procedures.** It is the responsibility or HR to put in place, and ensure **compliance** with, policies and procedures in respect of the above areas.

⑦ *Does HR represent staff and workers?*

This is an important question and the answer is "No". Despite possible appearances to the contrary, the role of HR is to represent the top management of the company in implementing policies and procedures and handling disputes.

⑦ *What makes good leaders and good managers?*

Leadership and management mean different things. However, leadership may involve management and management may involve leading a project or a group of people.

So what makes a good leader?

Essentially, good leaders need:

- **vision** – to see the future and its opportunities clearly, possibly more clearly than others.

- **decisiveness** – to make correct decisions quickly and not change their mind. Leaders are always well informed; and they select information from amongst many sources and interpret it carefully.

- **persuasiveness** – to convince others that their decision is right and that they should put it into action.

- **charisma** – the "X factor" which makes others naturally respect, obey, and follow them.

 ## *What's the difference between Leaders and Managers?*

Leaders set the overall strategy and direction of a company and, in so doing, make decisions which affect, either directly or indirectly, the amount of resources available in the company. The task of the **manager** is to **control** the use of these limited resources, and to maximum effect. Of course **management** may involve managing people, in a direct line relationship, but it may not: the resources managed may be materials, space or facilities, and they may also be people and situations external to the company.

So what makes a good manager?

Of course good managers come in all shapes and sizes, and may apply their own different form of personal magic. However, there are some simple basic qualities which make managers good managers:

- **effectiveness.** Effective managers affect (make a difference to) the organisation in which they work. To quote Peter Drucker, the American business educator and writer, "efficiency is doing things right; effectiveness is doing the right things".(4)

Efficiency is about doing things, yourself. Effectiveness is more about getting other people to do things. Peter Drucker states that to be effective is the job of the executive and that the executive is expected to get the right things done.(5)

- **decisiveness.** Like leaders, good managers have to make good decisions, often based on the best, but limited, information.

- **empowerment.** Good managers create the right circumstances in which to manage. They demand to be **empowered** and make it happen. Where possible they demand and obtain the required information, and the freedom and authority to make decisions based on it. Possibly the most important thing which affects an employee's performance, and in particular a manager's ability to manage, is his own direct superior. If the manager's superior withholds information, comprises his authority, or tries to manage his manager's work for him, the subordinate manager becomes disempowered, his task hopeless, and his credibility destroyed. Good managers, however, don't simply hope or wait for their superior to do the right things. They (diplomatically and carefully) demand the right treatment from their superiors.

- **proactive approach**. The culture in the UK is also not to wait for instruction – good managers understand the scope and authority of their role and perform **proactively** (which means they don't react to other people, or wait for other people to tell them what to do). They will inform their superior of their decisions and actions ('keep them in the loop'). So good managers take advantage of the power to make, and carry out, good decisions independantly, based on good information, which triggers actions by others.

- **persuasiveness.** As in the case of the leader, the manager operates effectively when he has the ability to get the people who report to him to believe that his decisions and the direction which he sets are right. He'll be careful as to how he does this, and he may occasionally 'bow' to the opinions of his subordinates, but he will not want to do this too often.

- **good organisation.** Good managers don't spend time trying to find things and don't have desks cluttered with paper. They don't forget meetings –

they manage a time organising system which works. Above everything, good managers organise their time with careful planning. They don't waste time because they know that it cannot be stored, or replaced, and that there is only one chance to spend it. They know that time is amongst their most valuable resources. So they guard it and cherish it, and they are quite decisive about not spending time at the wrong time or on unimportant things. They allow time for things to happen – good managers tend not to be late and in a rush. They plan their day.

- **calmness and control.** In addition to having control of their time, good managers create respect by appearing to be in control. They have authority and know what's going on, but they don't overreact to bad news, difficulties, or irritating behavior. They plan, where possible, or consider carefully, what they are going to do and say. They avoid strong and bad language, don't shout, and know that "less is more" both in speaking and in use of body language.

- **good presentation.** Good managers understand the importance of appearance. Nowhere more than in business is "perception reality". Simply stated, this means that *it is not enough to be good – a manager has to be seen to be good*. If he is perceived to be good, then, to a large degree, he is good. So, in general, the more senior a manager, the more appearance-conscience he is. Appearance is key to his effectiveness. Good managers are normally smart and well groomed: they don't wear the same shirt on consecutive days; they keep their office and their car clean and tidy; they don't have dirty shoes and fingernails.

  In addition, good managers take extreme care, and make enormous preparations, over presentations they have to make. They know that these have a high impact on how they are perceived. Good managers are normally articulate and have well-organised notes.

- **focus.** Here's another big business concept. Good managers *prioritise* and know exactly their agenda – they know exactly what they are trying to achieve. They deal with one thing at a time and they give that topic all their attention. They don't like digressions, don't get sidetracked, and they aren't constantly preoccupied with sending and receiving messages and trying to call people.

(?) *But what makes a good people manager?*

Well, these things:

- **ability to delegate**. Effective people managers don't do much: they get things done by other people. In order to maximise the effectiveness of this, they **empower** their staff by allocating "terms of reference" – authority, responsibility, and also **accountability** (which means that the person empowered not

---

I've experienced the effect of empowering management. I was recruited by the Chief Executive of the north-east region of a UK energy company with the task, among other things, of "changing the culture".

I saw the problem at the first Christmas party I attended. It resembled *The Night of the Walking Dead*. In the New Year, we set about the task for real. We really went for our policy of empowerment.

My boss had said to me, as he must have said to others: "Des , I'm now paying you the biggest compliment I can – I'm turning my back on you. These are your departments – you manage them. I'll not get involved. But these are the conditions:
- Don't bust your budget
- Don't break company policies and procedures
- Don't break the law
- And: if something goes seriously wrong, tell me
- Also: say the same thing to your own managers".

Our region became a high profile region. People said that you could almost touch the energy when you walked through the door. We headed the league table for debt collection (having been previously near the bottom). At the next year's Christmas party my boss had to stand on a table to get attention amid the hullabaloo.

In fact, it was a rather nondescript office in a rather nondescript area of Leeds, and they were just ordinary people working there. But what unbelievable energy and what an unbelievable atmosphere!

You really can change a culture, but it needs to be driven from the top.

---

only takes responsibility for decisions and actions, but also must justify his decisions and actions in the light of resulting mistakes and adverse consequences). Good managers set a clear direction and delegate complete, chunky tasks. They don't interfere. They create the conditions around the managed person for him to succeed. They ensure that the managed person has access to the required information, and, like soldiers in a jungle scything a route, attempt to remove obstacles from his path. Finally, they review progress regularly, as positively, objectively and unobtrusively as possible.

- **ability to motivate.** Managers motivate their people by ensuring that they have suitable pay and tools. Especially, they give them an opportunity to contribute to their agenda. They leave them to work unsupervised where possible and, although the manager may make suggestions and attempt to 'tweak' the direction their work is taking, they avoid telling them what to do. They indicate clearly, and as fully as possible, the "bigger picture" within which the people are working. They communicate regularly, and use formal mechanisms, for example the annual staff appraisal, to give their people a vision of how their work may lead to their advancement

- **ability to organise people.** Good managers have a skill at forming teams, so that the right people work together on the right things in a controlled way. Good managers also connect one activity to another so that, instead of work taking place in a vacuum, it assists, or is assisted by, something which is happening elsewhere in the company. A good manager acts rather like a radar scanner: he finds out what's going on in the company which is relevant to his team and to the team's area of operations. By making connections between activities or people he creates "**synergy**", where the result of combined activities is larger than the sum of the results of the individual component elements.

Sometimes managers inspire subordinates through their actions – through 'leading from the front'. Sometimes they inspire by the force of their personality or through a kind of personal magic. However, more frequently, they motivate their people by consistently giving them a vision of what they can achieve, or how they can contribute, rather than by doing any one thing in a particular way. Like most things in business, management consists of "ten per cent inspiration and 90 per cent perspiration", but the perspiration must be expended on the right things.

I've discussed the question of what makes a great manager a lot with experienced managers in my classes. Here's a list of the most frequently offered adjectives describing good and bad managers:

Figure 2.1 Adjectives describing good and bad managers

GOOD MANAGERS

empowering	available	open
assertive	honest	reasonable
decisive	consistent	human
persuasive	good at listening	discreet
approachable	objective	professional

BAD MANAGERS

volatile	uncommunicative	negative
dictatorial	aggressive	critical
two-faced	biased	workaholic

Marketing

We saw in Part 1 that the best method of operation, for a business organisation in a free market economy, is to offer to the market, in the form of supplying goods or providing services , that which the market is likely to want and buy. The diagram on page 17 indicates that companies do not produce, then try to find a buyer for their product. They produce for a buyer that they know, or believe exists. Marketing is the activity of creating potential buyers in the market place. It is the activity that prepares the company to offer the right things to the market, and which prepares the market to buy them.

Here's a definition of marketing:

Marketing attempts to understand the market and its requirements so that the company only provides products or services which the market wants. It creates demand within the market, thereby minimising the selling activity required.

? **_Phew! So, what is a "market"?_**

A market is the total demand for a particular product or service within a defined geographical and product area and/or group of potential customers.

Also, a market is the interaction of buyers and sellers in connection with a particular type of product or service.

A market, therefore, may, or may not be, a physical place. It may be a physical market, i.e. a collection of tables and stalls, or it may be the total activity of buying and selling commodities or financial services. It may, also, be the opportunity to sell, provided by demand for a product ("there's a fantastic market for this").

(?) *So, where does marketing start?*

An essential starting point in marketing, especially for new companies or companies offering new products, is **market research**. However, making enquiries in the market is difficult (or, as we should say in business, "challenging"), as a market consists of millions of individuals who do not always do what they say they'll do.

Companies research the market, in respect of existing products which already exist, in the following ways:

- **speaking to customers.** A key method of obtaining feedback is by sales assistants enquiring of customers, for example, in a clothing retailer like Marks and Spencer. Companies also use **focus groups** of customers who are paid to meet at the company and discuss the product.

- **questionnaires** are commonly used by companies to check the level of customer satisfaction of a service; for example, in a hotel or during a training course.

In respect of new companies, or companies with new products, market research most commonly takes three forms:

- **economic research** focuses on how wealthy people are, and how much, in comparison with previous years, they are spending in specific areas of the economy.

- **demographic research** focuses on consumers by age groups and their spending patterns.

- **research into competitors**, or potential competitors, may give the company information as to who the company is going to have to beat in respect of a particular product .

Let's take an example of these three forms of research. If a writer or company was considering introducing travel books into the market, research would show an enormous increase in travel in recent years, especially in respect of the over 50s age group. It may be possible to establish which the most popular destinations for these people are, and then what books already exist in respect of this particular market. The decision as to whether to go ahead with a proposed book, and in what form, would then be clearer.

 ## What is market segmentation?

The objective of market research is that a company chooses the most advantageous part, or **segment** of the market to attack. In the above example, the preferred segment might be relatively wealthy, older people wishing to take expensive breaks to major cities. This would then become the **target market** and the writer or company would choose this type of book in preference to a book focussing, for example, on cheaper, longer holidays aimed at younger people.

Companies always think in terms of the target market. It's extremely rare in business to produce something for everyone, and succeed. I guess the target market for this book is people between the ages of 16 and 25, either from the UK or not, who have ambitions to study business or enter the world of business. (If you've got a few grey hairs and are already well established in your career, please keep reading – I'm sure we can all learn from each other!).

It is, of course, critical that the company not only offers a product that the research suggests the market wants; the product must also be within the company's competence to supply, with a minimum of disruption and investment. This can become difficult to assess if, for example, the conclusion of the research is that the market is overseas.

So what does marketing consist of?

Once we have decided what products to produce or services to offer, the objective of marketing is to bring them to the attention of the customer in the most effective way. Marketing is about getting the customer, in a crowded and competitive market place, to buy the marketing organisation's products, and not those of its competitors. The customer's buying decision may be very quick (for example in a supermarket) and may be based on one or more small considerations. This could be called the **"marginal decision to buy"**. It could be argued that the result of the perfect marketing campaign is that the product sells itself.

Having chosen its segment and identified its target market, the company then attempts to create the marginal decision to buy within this market using what marketers call the "**marketing mix**".

(?) *What's the "marketing mix"?*

If you have studied business at all you no doubt have heard of the **four "P"s of marketing** which make up the marketing mix. Here they are displayed in Figure 2.2:

Figure 2.2 The four "P"s of marketing

PRICE	**P**ROMOTION
PLACE	**P**RODUCT

Let's take a few minutes minute to run through the four "P's" again:

Price
A company has two main options when considering how to price its product:

- Pricing based on the cost of supply. This can be called "**cost plus pricing**", where **cost + markup** (profit on one product) = price. This is normally used at the bottom end of the market , for example by budget **retailers** and sole traders or small organisations taking on jobs or contracts.

- Pricing according to what the market will bear. This can be called "**value added**" pricing and has the concept that the market will pay according to the perceived value **to the market**. Value added pricing applies in the case of property for sale or rent, and in retail generally at the higher price end of markets.

Clearly price is a key element in the "marginal decision to buy". Price can be used as a marketing tool and directed at the customer in the following ways:

- **direct comparison,** against a directly competing product;

- **reduction from the normal price** for the particular product. Such reduced prices are normally compared with the "**RRP**" (recommended retail price) which has at some time been charged for the product. These reductions come in the form of discounts offered at a sale, in an outlet store or special offers, e.g. **BOGOF** – "buy one get one free". There is, of course, psychology involved here: if I see that a shirt has been reduced from £59.99 to £35.00, then £35.00 appears to be a good price. Sometimes the reduction seems more important to the customer than the actual price paid. Prices today are so frequently discounted that the regular price becomes indistinct. Sales start before Christmas and the discount is from an already discounted price.

> I recently bought a brand new, state of the art camera at a leading electrical retailer – £99, reduced from £199. The camera failed almost immediately (I'm not very good with gadgets). When I tried to claim a replacement camera under the warranty for a value of £199, I was told that this price had no real significance. Interesting!

- **loss leader pricing** where one or more products are selected for sale at a specially reduced price in the hope of attracting sales at normal prices. Supermarkets, for example, advertise on a loss leader basis both on television and by distributing fliers to get customers into the stores.

- **prestige pricing** means charging a high price to give the product a prestigious image. Examples of a prestige pricing, in the UK beer market, could be

St Miguel or Peroni, where the pricing of the product reinforces the image of superiority or exclusivity. Prestige pricing may also be called **premium pricing**; so a prestige or premium-priced product is a **premium product**

Promotion

Promotion is any activity which brings the product to the attention of the potential buyer.

The main forms of promotion are:

- **advertising**, which may be on TV or radio, in newspaper and magazines, or **billboards** on a hoarding by the side of the road. Advertisements on TV or radio are called **commercials** and the word advertisement can be shortened to "**ad**". With the budget for a Guinness ad equalling that of an Oscar-winning film, it's clear that TV advertising has reached a new level, becoming highly-sophisticated, possibly a form of art. (If you're reading this as an overseas student living in the UK, check out the quality of TV and radio commercials – along with food retailing it's something that we do really well). Advertising may also be rather less obvious: there is a great deal of advertising of books, films and TV programmes done by television personalities who give interviews for magazines, appear on chat shows, or sit on the breakfast news sofa.

- **price promotion**, where a product is brought to the attention of the customer by means of a special offer on price together with special advertising and a prominent display of the product.

- **public relations (PR)**, which is when a company makes available news or information about itself to newspapers, magazines or TV.

- **sponsorship**, where an organisation pays money to have its name associated with an event, or series of events, (for example the Barclays Premier League in the UK).

- **endorsement**, where a famous person uses a product (e.g. a famous golfer wearing a "Nike" cap).

- **placement**, where a product is featured in a TV programme or film (e.g. the use of a BMW car in a James Bond film).

Place

The business word for place is "**location**". In marketing, "place" refers to the way in which the goods are physically positioned for sale. The facility where goods are sold to individual customers is an **outlet**. (If a store is an **outlet store**, this has the specific meaning that the goods in the store are being sold at a reduced price in order to move the product quickly).

   In **retailing** (selling goods to the general public), place is so important that there is a mantra:

Figure 2.3 The three important things in retailing

Location, location and **location!**

Place, or location, concerns three main items:

- the **type of outlet** in which the goods are sold.

- the **location of the outlet** in which the goods are sold. As an example, if the decision to buy is simply the result of walking past the outlet, rather than the decision being made in advance, it will be extremely important how many people walk past. This concept is known in retail as "**footfall**".

- the **position in the outlet** of the goods for sale (have you noticed how supermarkets position sweets at the checkout at the right height for children to grab?).

Product

A product is anything for sale which satisfies a customer. A product may not be physical. A **product may be a service** (a bank refers to a particular type of loan or financial service as a " product"). A product may be a famous person, a place or a building. It may be a can of beans or a made-to-measure suit. Anything which can be marketed and sold is a product.

There are four main areas to consider when discussing product:

- **specification** concerns the specific attributes or features of the product. If the product is a physical one then it concerns size, weight, strength and physical features. The specifications of a mobile phone, for example, might include the thickness, weight and screen size, and that of a beer the percentage alcohol by volume. If the product is a service the specifications might be the conditions for the **warranty, guarantee** or **after sales service**.

What's the difference between warranty and guarantee?

Technically there is probably no difference but in practice a warranty is often where the manufacturer promises to fix the product during the **warranty period** if it develops a fault. If it's a guarantee, the manufacturer will often replace the product with a new one. As the world of financial services has taken over from the manufacturing industry in the UK, warranties have become more complex and sophisticated, and should be considered carefully before purchase.

> When I bought my computer, the warranty which I ended up buying cost about 55% of the value of computer. When the computer failed after just over a year (as I said, I'm not very good with gadgets), I found that it only covered accidental damage, not parts failure. The only way to claim was to punch it or spill coffee over it! I needed, a new warranty cost a further 35% of the original price of the computer. It's important to ask the right question.

- **functionality** is about what the product can DO, so this normally refers to physical products. The functionality of a mobile phone is about whether it can send emails or take photographs, not how much it weighs or how sexy it looks!

- **appearance** probably sells products more than anything else, especially to the casual, non-technical buyer. To use beer as an example: it is clearly important that the beer has an attractive, possibly golden colour, and, in the north of England, brewers spend an enormous amount of money and effort ensuring the "head" – the froth at the top of the beer – is retained as the beer is drunk. In the case of physical products, this is often the responsibility of the design department. In the case of services, it is often no more than the style of the writing which supports the product – it's a good idea not to buy a warranty or any financial services product on the basis of the headline offer as the key "nasties" are often included in the **fine print**.

- **Quality** has different meanings: it can refer to the product's position in the market, for example BMW competes in the "quality" car market. Or it refers to the product's ability to perform the function for which it was designed. This is described on management courses as "fitness for purpose" – you may have a very cheap car but if it consistently does everything perfectly, as it should, then you can say that the quality is high. We'll look at quality in more detail later.

Is there a fifth "P" of Marketing?

Yes, marketers do sometimes refer to a fifth "P" :

Packaging is extremely important in marketing. It refers to the materials used to wrap or protect the goods. It can be used more generally to refer to the way in which the goods are presented to the customer for sale. Packaging can, alternatively, be included within "Product".

Packaging can have a dramatic effect on the sales performance of a product. Whether beer is sold in a can or a bottle, whether laundry liquid is sold in a bottle or a plastic box of capsules, whether a credit card deal is worded attractively (the fine print would definitely NOT be part of the packaging!) has a dramatic effect on the "marginal decision to buy".

The marketing mix is a combination which together forms a marketing campaign. It is not correct to think of marketing as a separate, standalone department. The marketing mix permeates the whole company and connects closely and continually with other functions, in particular finance (pricing), operations (product), and sales (presentation of the product and feedback on sales perfomance in different locations).

An example of using all the "P"s to remarket a product is the energy drink Lucozade. As a child, I was given Lucozade when I was sick. It was packaged in a glass bottle with a Cellophane wrap. It had a medicinal image. In 1983, the product was remarketed. The previous logo, "Lucozade aids recovery" was replaced with "Lucozade replaces lost energy". Now the product range has been extended to include different flavours. It has been advertised as a sports/health drink on a TV commercial featuring a famous athlete. It has been repackaged in a sporty bottle with an attractive label. It competes on price with other health/sports drinks; it is available in vending machines and in the typical outlets where young, sporty health-conscious consumers would buy such a drink. In short, the marketers have completely transformed the image of the drink, using all the elements of the marketing mix.

Of course products are now sold increasingly on the internet. Most people have access (place), websites are clear (promotion), delivery times short and the returns process normally easy (product) and prices low, due to reduction of selling costs. (Try comparing the price of a printer ink cartridge with non-internet suppliers.)

(?) *What are the main marketing strategies?*

A large part of marketing is about creating a decision to buy amongst marginal customers. The marketing strategy will differ according to the marketing opportunity which exists. Philip Kotler (6), the distinguished American Professor of Marketing, identifies three sources of market opportunity:

- supplying something in short supply;

- supplying an existing product or service in a new way;

- supplying a new product or service.

If the market has competing products but is not full (or **saturated**), there being surplus demand for the product type, then the company may still introduce a competing product. Assuming the company gets the marketing mix right, there is no reason why the new product will not sell in addition to the existing products.

If no product exists, the company may decide to bring out a new product onto the market – this is called "**product innovation**". (Innovation is about making something work commercially – it's a bit more than **creativity**, which is simply about having ideas). If the market itself is not perceived to exist then the company may try to create a new market – "**market innovation**". An example of a new market being created for a new product is the Sony Walkman – people had never previously listened to music whilst jogging.

If the market is already saturated with competing products then the company will have to find a way of making its product more attractive to the customer than that of the competitors. It will need to introduce a **Unique Selling Proposition (USP)**.

What's a "Unique Selling Proposition"?

The **USP** is some unique quality about the company's product which will attract an indifferent customer to buy it in preference to a competitor's product in an adequately supplied market. It is what drives his marginal decision to buy. Any of the "P's" of the marketing mix can provide a competitive advantage: the product may be cheaper, better, more attractively packaged or better advertised.

So, here in Figure 2.4 is a summary of basic marketing strategies:

Figure 2.4 Basic marketing strategies

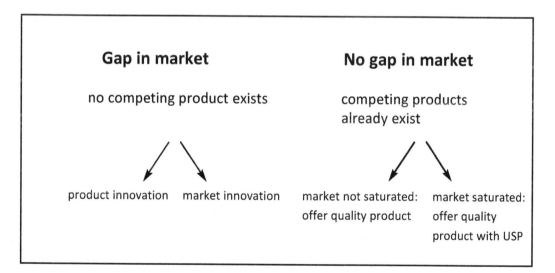

As the rate of change in the businesss environment quickens and intensifies, a company's ability to innovate, either in terms of introducing new products or changing existing ones, becomes ever more critical. Kotler makes the point that "successful companies seek to get all their departments to be customer-oriented, if not customer-driven."(7)

The innovation process is risky as market research is difficult and market behaviour unpredictable. Wikipedia provides the information that "Research findings vary, ranging from fifty to ninety percent of innovation projects judged to have made little or no contribution to organizational goals." One survey regarding product innovation quotes that "out of three thousand ideas for new products, only one becomes a success in the marketplace".(8)

An example of fierce competition is laundry detergent. Every aspect of the marketing mix seems to have been employed over the years to provide a competitive edge – in the area of product alone, what started as a white powder became a blue powder, compressed powder tablets, liquid tablets and liquid in a bottle. Applications include "whites" to "colour" to "bio" to "non-bio".

The balancing of risk, especially the risk of doing nothing, and reward in respect of innovation is a key aspect of the company's strategy. More on this later. One of the reasons companies innovate is in order to achieve a USP.

Companies use all five elements of the marketing mix in the hope of achieving a USP which they hope will persuade the marginal customer to buy. Finding a place in the market at which the product will be attractive to the customer is called **product positioning**.

Of course, price is important – whether the product is positioned as "upmarket", "economy" or "mid range". However, the company needs to use the other "P's" of the mix in order to achieve **product differentiation**.

Examples of product differentiation in the car market, listed in Figure 2.5, could be:

Figure 2.5 Product differentiation in the car market

More reliable	(VW)
Safer	(Volvo)
Technologically more advanced	(Audi)
Sexier	(Alfa Romeo)
Smaller	(Smart Car)

Branding

The attributes of a product, including its packaging and name, are brought together for presentation to the customer as a **brand**. A brand was originally an identifying mark made on the skin of a man or animal by hot metal to indicate ownership. Now it is the name by which a company makes its product recognisable and attractive to the customer. The brand name, reinforced by advertising, communicates certain messages or images to the customer about the product. The objective of the company is to build a brand which is so strong that the customer will select the brand in preference to other competing brands.

> At a computer company where I worked in the eighties, almost every male smoker bought Marlborough cigarettes. The image of the cigarettes was connected to a masculine, tough, outdoor life which appeared to suit the self-image of the male employee – it appeared that this affected the mass choice much more than taste or price.

A company may use a brand to convey many different aspects of the product, but to be effective all brands should be:

- **distinctive** – stands out in some way amongst the competing products.

- **consisent** – aways the same and therefore reliable.

- **recognisable** – for example, by the shape of the product or the packaging.

- **attractive**.

The position and differentiation of the product is reinforced by branding. A brand is much more than a name. Through advertising and the other "P"s of the marketing mix the brand becomes associated with a differentiated product and one with a particular position in the market. This positioning and differentiation which gives the product its USP is continually reinforced.

MacDonald's is clearly positioned at the inexpensive end of the food market (price) but the brand also conveys association in the mind of the customer. What does MacDonald's mean in your country? In the UK, it represents fun, bright lights and young staff. It's clearly strongly aimed at kids and teenagers. It also represents cleanliness. In a society neurotic about kids health, if you take your kids for a messy meal it's important that there are visual indicators of cleanliness: self-service bins, staff always cleaning, and spotless toilets.

The brand also represents great locations. You've got to hand it to MacDonald's: they really do know how to score on this "P". Across the world MacDonald's operate in central strategic and feature locations (check out the one next to the western station in Budapest). Of course, one of the most powerful tools for reinforcing brand positioning and differentiating is advertising. MacDonald's TV advertising in the UK normally emphasises price, but the logo, the golden arches which form an "M", seems to reinforce the idea of fun and brightness.

Not only do brands stand for price position or some form of product differentiation, they also stand for values. Values can be reinforced by advertising, for example the Hovis bread TV ad reinforced Britishness, and the Waitrose TV ad emphasised quality and acceptable food sourcing sold at a fair price. When a company achieves successful brand association, brand reinforcement and brand values in respect of their product, it hopes to gain **brand loyalty**: where a customer always prefers the brand of the company against that of a competitor.

If a company achieves powerful brand recognition in the market it can stretch the brand. **Brandstretching** is where a brand name, originally associated with one product or service, is extended to cover new brands or services. An example of brandstretching is where UK supermarket companies like Tesco have moved beyond food retailing into selling clothes, household goods and financial services. Banks have also moved from traditional banking activities, handling deposits and granting loans, to providing a window into a complete range of financial services at a competitive price, thereby offering the customer the convenience of "**one stop shopping**".

In summary, marketing, with the elements of the marketing mix, forms the basis of the company's response to its challenges. Typically, these are fierce competitor activity, the quickening development of technology, and constantly changing environments, markets and customer behaviour.

Finance

Introduction to Finance

If a company were a football team, the sales and marketing function would be the forwards and the finance function would be the backline. Because finance is not directly concerned with selling ("scoring goals"), but is more of a "backroom" operation, it has a rather unexciting image. However, a good finance department is an essential element of a successful company. The finance function includes accounting, which is the production and interpretation of financial statements from the transactions of the business. Accounting normally has its own department(s) and manager(s).

 What does the finance function do?

A good way of describing the finance function is to make a broad split between activities which have a focus external to the company and activities with a focus internal to the company as categorised in Figure 2.6:

Figure 2.6 Finance function activities

External Focus:	Internal Focus:
Financial Accounting	Cash Management

Tax Management	Management Accounting:
	    Internal Reporting
	    Costing
	    Budgeting and Forecasting
	    Capital Spend Appraisal

Financial Public Relations External Audit	Payroll Internal Audit

Let's look at these one by one.

"External focus" finance operations

Financial accounting
The following are the major financial accounting activities:

- **accounts payable:** the operation of paying suppliers in respect of purchases.

- **accounts receivable:** the opposite financial operation, that of collecting payment in respect of sales which the company has made. This is sometimes called "**collections**".

- **invoicing:** the financial operation of recording a sale and sending an invoice to the customer.

- **producing external financial statements:** all the financial transactions, in respect of sales and purchases, are recorded in the accounting system and fed into the summary system from which the required financial statements are produced. The summary accounting system is called the "**general ledger**". Because the **bookkeeping** of all the financial transactions involves double entry – that is a debit and a credit – the system produces a "**trial balance**", to prove that the debit totals and the credit totals agree. Assuming they do, the system will then be used to produce the three financial statements required for external presentation and registration. These three statements are:

- The Profit and Loss Account.

- The Balance Sheet.

- The Funds Flow Statement.

"**Financial Accounting**" is the name given to the accounting in respect of transactions between the company and the outside world. Also, it's the name given to the production, and registration with the authorities, of the financial statements which reflect those transactions. The UK authority which controls the registration of companies and their official returns is called "Companies House".

It's really important to understand these statements, as they are absolutely key to business finance. Let's have a look at them, and the terminology surrounding them.

Please note that the statements shown below are simplified for clarity. They do not represent any required reporting format.

The Profit and Loss Account

The Profit and Loss Account ("P&L") is a calculation of the result, in terms of the difference between the value in (sales value and other income value) and the cost value of business transactions conducted by the company during a period of time. This period is normally a year and is called the "**trading period**". It's very important to understand right at the start that the profit and loss account is about positive and negative values of recorded business transactions resulting in inflows and outflows of **value.** *It is not the same as receipts and payments of cash.*

Imagine you buy a product without actually paying for it, for £50, and agree to pay for it next month. You then sell it for £100 and agree to receive payment in two months' time. You are, in other words, conducting business on **credit**. Now you produce a profit and loss account. Your profit and loss account would show:

	£
Sales	100
Cost of sales	(50)
Profit	50

You have made £50 profit even though you have not paid or received any cash. It is the first essential rule of business finance that profit is not the same as cash.

A word about sales:

Value inflow from sales is called "**revenue**". The difference between revenue and income is that revenue is income generated by the company's product or service, whereas income is simply received from another organisation. "Sales" is therefore "revenue" and "bank interest" is "income". Sales revenue is often referred to as "**turnover**".

⊘ What's the difference between "sales" and "turnover"?

Sales represents the revenue received from any items sold by the company, whereas turnover is revenue received from sales of *what the business is in busi - ness to sell*. If, for example, a clothing retailer sells a company vehicle, this is not "turnover", because the company is not in business to sell vehicles. "Turnover" is also the total value of sales made in a complete trading period, and in respect of the whole company. Companies refer to sales made to one particular customer, or of one particular product, as "sales", not "turnover".

(?) *What are net sales?*

Net sales are:

Total sales made at normal price (sometimes called "gross sales")
less   discounts
less   reductions in respect of damaged goods or goods lost in transit to the customer
less   returns form customers of unwanted goods

Sometimes the calculation from gross sales to net sales is shown in the Profit and Loss Account. If not, and only one line item is shown in respect of sales, then the value will be that of net sales.

Now a word about profit:

Profit is the total surplus of a company's value inflow over its value outflow during a trading period. Profit can only be made by "for profit" organisations. ("Not for profit" organisations, or non-business organisations, cannot make a profit. Instead they make either a **surplus** or a **deficit**.)
   Unfortunately, the words used to describe profit cause confusion (so feel free to skip the next bit).

Profit can be calculated at different levels:

"**Gross profit**" is sales revenue less cost of sales, whilst
"**Net profit**", or "**profit after tax**" is the final "bottom line" calculation. This is:

Gross profit, less selling and administration Expenses, adjusted for interest and tax

(However, be careful: in the U.S. the word "income" is used to mean "profit", the net result of value in less value out. In the UK "income" is a value inflow to the company from an external organisation such as a bank or an investment).

Back in the UK, the words "profit" and "earnings" are used interchangeably. "Earnings" is operating revenue less total operating expenses. The key profit line which indicates earnings – the profit performance of the business from its operations – is **operating profit**:

Operating Profit   = Operating revenue less total operating expenses
                           = Earnings before interest and tax ("EBIT")

Operating profit, or earnings before interest and tax, is later adjusted by interest, tax receipts and payments, to arrive at final profit, normally referred to as "Profit after tax" in the UK.

(?) *What about "margin"?*

The word "**margin**" refers to the ratio of profit to sales, either for the whole company or part of it, so:

Gross Margin % =   Gross Profit X 100
                                     Sales

and

Net Margin % =   Profit After Tax X 100
                                     Sales

Finally, a word about depreciation:

Depreciation is the term we give to the reduction in value that takes place in a physical asset over time, either because of usage ("wear and tear"), obsolescence, or simply because the asset becomes older. Depreciation also refers to the charge which is made against profit to reflect this reduction of an asset's value (if the asset value reduces on the left hand side of the balance sheet , it must be "mirrored" by an equivalent reduction on the right hand side).

It's important to be clear that depreciation does not involve cash – the company is not putting cash, with which to buy a new asset, anywhere, but is simply recording accurately the fact that the reduction in asset value is a cost to the business. This is because the asset will eventually have to be replaced if the company is to continue. We call depreciation a "non-cash item", but it's as much a cost as a cash item such as heating.

Here in Figure 2.7 is an example of a **"proforma"** (without numbers) Profit and Loss Account:

Figure 2.7 A 'proforma' Profit and Loss Account

Sales minus: **Cost of sales**	Cost of sales is all costs directly linked to sales. These may be purchased goods which are then sold, or they may be goods which are manufactured by the company for sale , in which case all direct materials and direct labour costs will be included.
= **Gross profit** minus : **Overheads**	Overheads are expenses which are not directly linked to sales. Examples might be energy costs or directors' salaries
= **(Net) profit before interest and tax**	= "Earnings before Interest and Tax" (EBIT) Profit at this level is often called "operating profit" because it represents the profit which the company has made on its trading operation. This profit does not include bank interest, tax or other "extraordinary items" which are not reflective of the company's operating performance
plus/minus: **Interest**	Normally relates to interest paid to or received from a bank
= **Profit before tax** minus **Tax**	Sometimes referred to as "Earnings before Tax" (EBT).
= **Profit after tax**	Sometimes referred to as "Earnings after Tax" (EAT). This is the 'bottom line' profit which is the final calculation of profit made by the organisation in the trading period for the shareholders. It can be either distributed to shareholders or kept (retained) in the business for future use. Because it can be distributed this profit can be called "distributable profit".
minus **Dividend**	= Repayment of profit to shareholders
= **Retained profit**	= Profit kept in the business for future use

The Balance Sheet

Whereas the Profit and Loss Account covers the whole of a trading period and so is 'for the period ended …' the Balance Sheet relates to a moment in time, normally the end of the trading period. It is a "count-up" of the what the business *owns* (including what is owed to the business) – its "assets"; and what the business *owes* – its "liabilities".

Here's a "proforma" balance sheet (Figure 2.8):

Figure 2.8 A 'proforma' balance sheet

Assets		£	Liabilities		£
Fixed Assets	to be held for at least a year		**Long-term Liabilities**	not due to be repaid within a year	
Land and buildings			Bank Loan		
Equipment			Taxation Owed		
Vehicles					
Current Assets	to be turned into cash within a year		**Current Liabilities**	due to be repaid within a year	
Stock	inventory		Bank Loan		
Debtors	money owed by customers		Creditors	money owed to Suppliers	
Cash	includes bank deposits				
			Shareholders Funds	"equity capital"	
			Issued Share Capital	original contribution from shareholders	
			Reserves	retained profits + increases in value of business	

Notice that the assets, which the company owns, are grouped according to how 'liquid' they are – i.e. how quickly they can be converted into cash. The main division is between **"fixed assets"** – those which are likely to be owned by the business for at least a year before being turned into cash – and its "**current assets**" – those which will be converted into cash inside a year.

Within the fixed and current categories the individual assets are listed in order of liquidity, with the most "liquid" at the bottom and the most "illiquid" at the top. So in the "fixed assets" category, land and buildings is at the top because they are not likely to be turned into cash anytime soon. However, in the "current assets" category, bank and cash are at the bottom because they are already cash – that means they are totally liquid. Liabilities which must be repaid within a year are in "**current liabilities**", but, unfortunately for students, those which will remain unpaid for more than a year are not called "fixed" but "**long-term liabilities**".

The difference between the total value of the assets and the total values of the liabilities is the value of the business – what it could ("on paper") be sold for. This is the "**asset value**" of the business, also known as its "**net worth**". This figure is the same as the "**equity capital**" of the business, which is owned by the shareholders.

Capital
"**Capital**" is the money which finances the business long-term. If all the capital belongs to the shareholders then it is called "equity capital".

Why is "equity capital" (= "shareholders funds"), which is financing the company, on the liabilities side of the balance sheet?

The answer to this is that the money is not owned by the company, but is **owed** by the company to the owners. In the event that the business were sold, all the equity capital would be returned to the shareholders.

Capital may, however, be borrowed, often from a bank, in which case it is called "**debt capital**". If money is borrowed, it's only called "debt capital" if it's for the **long-term financing of the business**.

Whilst possibly appearing confusing, the following formulas in Figure 2.9 are essential to understanding the capital aspect of business finance.

Figure 2.9 The capital aspect of business finance

assets – liabilities	=	equity capital = net worth = net assets
assets – liabilities, which are not borrowed specifically for long-term financing	=	equity capital + debt capital

The equity capital, which belongs to the shareholders is often called "**shareholders funds**". It consists of two elements:

- **Issued share capital** (money contributed by shareholders);

- **Reserves** (profit or increase in the value of the company's assets since its start date, which also belongs to the shareholders).

Capital Gearing

Capital Gearing, called "**leverage**" in the US, simply refers to how large a proportion of a company's capital is is held in the form of debt. Generally, if the equity portion is less than half, the company is said to be "**highly geared**". If it's more than half, the company is said to be "**low geared**".

Funds Flow Statement

The Funds Flow Statement is also called:
- The "Cash Flow Statement" and
- The "Statement of Sources and Applications of Funds".

⑦ *What does the Funds Flow Statement Do?*

I pointed out earlier that profit represents the surplus of the "value in" over the "value out" in respect of a trading period of a business. This is not the same as cash. The Funds Flow Statement shows the **effect on cash** of the operations of the business during the trading year. Simply stated, this will be the bottom line profit adjusted for any transactions which did not involve receipt or payment of money. To take our earlier example, where no cash changed hands:

Figure 2.10 Simple example of bottom line profit

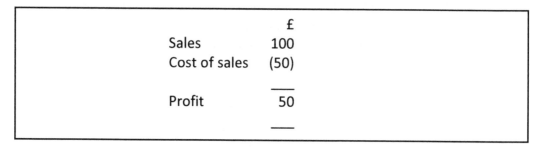

	£
Sales	100
Cost of sales	(50)
Profit	50

The Funds Flow Statement would show the difference between the profit position of 50 and the cash position of zero:

Figure 2.11 Simple example of funds flow statement

	£	
Profit	50	
add		
Increase in Creditors	50	(people we've not paid)
deduct		
Increase in Debtors	100	(people who've not paid us)
Total Cash Effect	0	

Simply stated, the cash effect shown in the Funds Flow Statement represents the profit, adjusted in respect of two different things:

- any line items in the profit and loss account which are non-cash items (for example depreciation of fixed assets or provision for debts which may not be paid).

- any increase or decrease in the value of balance sheet items between the balance sheet at the start of the trading period, and the balance sheet at the end of the trading period. These increases or decreases are equivalent to payments or receipts of cash. For example:

- an increase in equipment would represent cash paid;
- an increase in debtors would represent cash not received (= same effect as cash paid);
- an increase in creditors would represent cash not paid (= same effect as cash received).

Taking these factors into account Figure 2.12 offers a less simple example of a proforma Funds Flow Statement.

Figure 2.12 Example of a 'proforma' funds flow statement

		£
Net Profit		
<u>Add</u>	Depreciation	
	Increase in provisions	
	Increase in creditors	
		———
<u>Deduct</u>	Increase in motor vehicles	
	Increase in debtors	
		———
Total change in cash		
		———

Because the changes in the values in the two balance sheets are needed to construct the Funds Flow Statement, the closing balance sheet should be completed first. Also, only when the closing balance sheet is completed can the change in the cash position be verified.

A worked example of the three financial accounts

You and I decide to start a business on 1 January 2011. Before we start, we do the following:

- We each contribute £15,000 capital to the business;
- We raise a bank loan of £10,000;
- We buy a building for £30,000 and equipment for £10,000.

Our opening balance sheet will look like this:

OPENING BALANCE SHEET (as at 1 January 2011)

	£		£
Buildings	30,000	Loan	10,000
Equipment	10,000		
		Shareholders Funds	30,000
	40,000		40,000

During our first year of business we make the following transactions:

	£	
We buy goods for £60,000, but we still owe	6,000	at 31/12/2011
We sell goods for £85,000 but we are still owed	8,000	at 31/12/2011
We purchase, for cash, another building for	5,000	
We spend money on running the business the during the year of 2011	12,000	
We provide for taxation (but don't pay it)	4,000	
We pay interest on the bank loan	500	
We have goods in stock at the end of the year, which we purchased during the year of	5,000	

We decide to make no charge for depreciation of fixed assets.

Our cash is affected as follows:

	£		£
Opening cash balance	0	Payment for property	5,000
Sales receipts for year	77,000	Payment for goods	54,000
(85,000 – 8,000)		(60,000 – 6,000)	
		Expenses	12,000
		Bank interest	500
Closing cash balance	**5,500**		

Our Profit and Loss Account will look like this:

PROFIT AND LOSS ACCOUNT for the Year ended 31 December 2011

	£
Sales	**85,000**
Cost of goods sold:	
purchases	(60,000)
less closing stock	5,000
Cost of goods sold:	**(55,000)**
Gross profit	**30,000**
Expenses	(12,000)
(Net) Profit before interest and tax	**18,000**
(= EBIT = Operating profit)	
Bank interest	(500)
Profit before tax (= PBT = EBT)	**17,500**
Tax provision	(4,000)
Profit after tax (= PAT = EAT)	**13,500**
Dividend	0
Retained profit	**13,500**

CLOSING BALANCE SHEET (as at 31 December 2011)

	£	£		£	£
Fixed Assets			**Long-term Liabilities**		
Buildings		35,000	Loan		10,000
Equipment		10,000			
Current Assets			**Current Liabilities**		
Stock	5,000		Creditors	6,000	
Debtors	8,000		Tax	4,000	10,000
Cash	5,500	18,500			
			Equity Capital		
			Issued share capital	30,000	
			Retained profit	13,500	43,500
		63,500			63,500

FInally, our Funds Flow Statement will show the following effects:

FUNDS FLOW STATEMENT (for the year ended 31 December 2011)

Sources (+)	£	Applications (-)	£
Retained Profit	13,500	New buildings	5,000
Creditors	6,000	Debtors	8,000
Tax	4,000	Stock	5,000
Increase in Cash:	5,500		

This statement explains why, when we have a **retained profit** of £13,500, our **cash** has only increased by £5,500.

The Annual Report

It is requirement of a UK legally registered company to publish an annual report. The Annual Report contains the three financial reports we've already looked at. In addition, it must contain further information. The total information which is required by law, which includes information to be included in the three financial statements, is referred to as the "**disclosure requirements**" and also includes:

- Notes to the Accounts
- Directors' Report
- Auditors' Report

Tax management

The Financial Director needs to find the correct balance between the following:

- reporting the maximum profit for the organisation;
- giving the best representation of the company to the outside world; and
- optimising the company's tax position (which will, of course, be based on the amount of profit the company makes).

The tax rules are extremely complicated and the Finance Director may need to take advice from an external tax advisor. There are two key concepts in relation to tax:

- **tax avoidance** is finding a way of making tax not payable and often involves the help of external tax advisers. Tax avoidance is legal.
- **tax evasion** is deliberately not paying tax which is payable. Tax evasion is illegal and carries strict penalties.

The name given to tax on a company's profit in the UK is "**corporation tax**".

Financial public relations

An important role of the Finance Director of a public limited company is to manage public relations with external people. These may be actual or potential investors, the stock market, or the banks. This is essentially done by "talking up" the company's performance in general and in terms of profit in particular. There are two basic objectives of these financial public relations:

- To maximise the amount of investment into the company by shareholders.

- To maximise the market value of the shares for the shareholders, and therefore the market value of the company. The higher the share value climbs, the higher the market value of the company. This is also called the "**market capitalisation**".

External measurements

These are measurements which are frequently reported by companies to their shareholders and to external institutions, and which have a significant impact on the way the company is perceived.

("The word "**return**" refers to profit expressed as a percentage of something else. So profit = **earnings** = return.)

Frequently used measurements are identified in Figure 2.14:

Figure 2.13 Frequently used measurements

Earnings per share	=	$\dfrac{\text{profit after tax}}{\text{number of shares in issue}}$
Return on equity	=	$\dfrac{\text{profit after tax}}{\text{total equity capital}} \times 100\%$
Price/earnings ratio	=	$\dfrac{\text{market price of share}}{\text{earnings per share}}$

"Return on equity" shows how efficiently the directors are managing their shareholders' investment. The first two measurements, therefore, concern profitability. The third is a measure of how highly investors rate the profit which a company has produced.

External audit

It is a requirement of all UK limited companies that they are externally audited. This means that the statements produced for external reporting are checked for accuracy and compliance against an accounting regulation by an external firm of accountants.

(?) What are the objectives of an external audit?

The objectives of an external audit are to:

- provide protection to the company's shareholders, or potential share-holders, against the company's financial situation, and therefore value, being misrepresented;

- give reassurance to the company's directors that the financial numbers and the accounting systems are OK ("have **integrity**") and that the tax position, which the Finance Director will have tried to optimise, is legitimate;

- provide reassurance to the general public that the company is meeting its public tax obligations.

(?) What's the finished product of an external audit?

The finished product of an external audit is an Audit Report. This must be included in the company's Annual Report. The best result for the company is an 'unqualified report'. This does not mean that the auditors are not qualified to give an opinion, but that their opinion has no qualification – which means no serious negative aspect. An unqualified report means three things:

- that the figures are not significantly wrong (or to use auditor speak, "**materially misstated**").

- that they are produced in accordance with the prevailing accounting rules or "**convention**" (in the UK this is **UK GAAP – Generally Accepted Accounting Principles**). Figures may also have to comply with "**IAS – International Accounting Standards**".

- that the audit process has been complete and not restricted in any way.

Internal finance operations

Cash management

It is vital that a company generates enough **cash**, and not only profit, to continue its operations. Profit does not pay for suppliers, salaries and other company needs, but cash does. The Finance Director must manage the company's overall cash situation. In practice this means he must manage closely:

- the current assets, which will be turned into cash as the company continues to operate (normally stock and debtors).

- the current liabilities which will require payment in cash – in particular trade creditors and the amounts due to the tax authorities.

The surplus of current assets over current liabilities, (**net current assets**), is known as **working capital** or **liquidity**.

One of the main reasons for company failure is lack of working capital, so the control of cash is one of the key contributions of the finance function to the company. The generation and usage of cash due to the operations of the business is called **cash flow** and the **Cash Flow Forecast** is one of the Finance Director's most important planning tools.

Internal reporting

In the UK, the whole area of internal control and reporting is normally called **Management,** or **Managerial, Accounting** Elsewhere In Europe, it is often called "**Controllership**". In essence, management accountants provide information to the company's management ("**management information**"), to inform them as to how well the business is performing financially. Managers need to know the performance for the whole company and for individual parts or products of the business – they need to know which parts or products are winners or losers financially.

> Numbers have little meaning when not compared to other numbers. So, one of the first rules of producing business information is that it should be relative. I could say, for example, that in 2007/8 serious or fatal injuries in the UK due to the use of firearms were 455. The information has more impact if I say that this was 3% less than the previous year. It has considerably more impact if I say that total murders using firearms in the US in 2005 was 10,000.

? What's the difference between a budget and a forecast?

A **budget** is normally an estimate or target of performance for a year. A **forecast** is an estimate or target in respect of any other period of time – a company may have a six-month forecast or a five-year forecast. A budget may be called an annual **plan**. Budgets and forecasts may relate to volume or units, for example of production, or may relate to money.

Typically a company finalises its annual budget in August/September for a year running from January to December. As the year progresses, say from winter to spring, the company replace or supplement its budget with a forecast for the remaining part of the year. The forecast may then become more important to the company than the budget.

A "**projection**", sometimes called an "**outlook**", is normally an estimate further into the future, based on less scientific and more arbitrary assumptions.

The numbers relating to the performance which in fact happens are called "**actual**", or sometimes "**historical**". It's very important that budgets, forecasts and especially actuals are available at the right time and do not become out of date or "yesterday's news". One of the practical problems in the past with recording "actuals" was that they took time to be calculated, so that by the point the monthly figures were available and checked they were too late to be of much use. Often the accountant would be pressed to produce a "**flash**" (the latest estimated "actual" based on the latest figures available) earlier than the real results, and whilst actually trying to calculate them. Now that computers generate real time information, the reporting of actuals is much quicker. However, it's not unusual for accountants to be pressured to release figures to management before they are checked and finalised.

(?) *What's Included in a budget or forecast?*

The actual detail of what's included in the budget or forecast varies from company to company, but normally includes the calculation of the profit (sales and other income less costs). This can be included both in summary form and with the relevant departments calculating the detail of each supporting line. The calculated difference between the actual and budget or forecast is called the "**variance**". Often the budget or forecast forms a twelve-monthly "**spread**". When two or more months actual results are known, they can be totalled to give a "**year to date**" or "**cumulative**". The full year will project a mixture of actual achieved plus the forecast for the rest of the year, together with a comparison against budget.
    Here's a simple example:

Figure 2.14 Simple example of profit forecast

	Profit Forecast 2011														
	January			February			March			April – December			Full Year		
	Bud	Act	Var	Bud	Act	Var	Bud	Act	Var	Bud	Fcast	Var	Bud	Fcast	Var
Sales	100	102	2	90	89	-1	95	98	3	900	910	10	1185	1199	14
Costs	-90	-91	-1	-80	-81	-1	-86	-87	-1	-90	-89	1	-346	-348	-2
Profits	10	11	1	10	8	-2	9	11	2	810	821	11	839	851	12

Actually setting a budget or forecast can be a tricky exercise. If the figures are supplied by more junior people actually doing the job, when the budget is totalled it will not give the result required by senior management. However, if the budget is simply set at the top of the company, it will not have the **ownership** of the people who will carry it out. Budget and forecast processes, therefore have to be a combination of a "**bottom up**" and "**top down**" process so that the right result is achieved *and* has the **commitment** of people lower down the organisation.

Internal measurements

We have already talked about external measurements. Let's now look at a few ways of measuring **internal performance**:

- **Liquidity ratio:**
  $$\frac{\text{Current assets less stock}}{\text{Current liabilities}}$$

The company's liquidity concerns how easily it can pay its day to day running costs. Normally "liquid" assets are cash and bank balances, other "money" (for example in the form of bills receivable and quoted securities), and trade debtors. In other words, they are cash, or items which can be turned into cash, in the ordinary course of business without serious inconvenience, and, in the case of debtors, within the normal time allowed for payment to the company. Stocks, which can be less easily converted into cash, are not included.

    The balance sheet figure for liquid assets is compared to the amount owing in respect of day to day running costs. If the ratio is less than 1.0, the company probably has insufficient liquidity.

- **Stock Days:**
  $$\frac{\text{Stock}}{\text{Purchases}} \times 365$$

This ratio compares total cost of purchases for the year (used to provide sales) with the closing stock of purchased items held. If purchases are 1200 and closing stock 200, then the company has stock for two months' operation. The lower the stock days, the more efficiently the company is using its stock.

- **Debtors Days:**
  $$\frac{\text{Debtors}}{\text{Sales}} \times 365$$

In this ratio closing Debtors in the balance sheet (money owed to the company in respect of sales) is compared to sales for the year. This is a measure of the number of days that the company takes to collect money from debtors. The lower the figure, the more efficiently the company is collecting its debt.

- **Creditors Days:**
  $$\frac{\text{Creditors}}{\text{Purchases}} \times 365$$

This is the opposite of debtors payment period. Here, closing creditors in the balance sheet are compared to total purchases for the year. This measures the number of days that the company takes to pay suppliers. The higher the figure, the better the company's cash position will be.

- **Return on Sales:** $\dfrac{\text{Profit before interest and tax}}{\text{Total sales}} \times 100\%$

This compares the operating profit with sales, over a period of one year. It shows how efficiently the directors are using the sales revenue to manage costs and overhead, and to drive the business forward. The higher the result, the stronger the company will be to handle problems such as price wars, increasing costs, or reducing sales.

A couple more points in connection to company measurements:

- The exact definitions, for example "capital employed", and therefore the exact calculations, can vary from company to company.

- Measuring company performance is a relatively long-term activity and the **trend** – comparison of several years' sequential results – is normally more representative than one year's results only.

Costing
One of the simple questions which companies face is:

How much does everything, which the company does or makes, cost? Of course, when a company produces its Profit and Loss Account, all the costs and expenses are included. However, this account is only produced once a year, and it relates to the whole company. Costing, which normally takes place in production companies, involves the calculation and reporting of the different parts of the company as soon as possible after the production has taken place and the costs have been incurred. Many companies, for example, produce a cost report every month.
Costs are normally split in the following ways:

- Between **direct costs** (i.e. costs directly connected to production, such as direct labour and materials) and **indirect costs,** such as cleaning and company vehicle costs

- Between production processes and product costs.

- Between **variable costs** (direct costs which are directly proportionate to the amount of units produced) and **fixed costs** (indirect costs, such as overhead costs, which are incurred even if nothing is produced). Products whose price covers all their variable costs, and part of the fixed costs which are allocated to them, are said to be making a "**contribution**". Cost analysis based on the differentiation between fixed and variable costs is called "**marginal costing**"

If a company knows how much its product costs, and knows its production process costs, and its fixed and variable costs, then it will be able to calculate, report, and control its performance in terms of efficiency. It will be able to analyse where, in terms of products and processes, it is winning and losing. This is another way in which Finance can make a major contribution to the company.

Sometimes cost targets, or standards, are set and reported against. This is called "**standard costing**".

Costing can help a company in the following ways:

- companies can use costing to price their products at a level which produces a profit.

- "marginal costing" can help companies to know how much of a product must be produced before the company makes a profit.

- "marginal costing" can also help companies can make a better decision as to whether or not to continue to produce a product which appears to be making a loss.

Because marginal costing connects closely to production, there's more on marginal costing in the next section on "Operations".

Capital spend
An important element in cash flow forecasting is the control of capital spend.

(The words 'capital' and 'revenue' are amongst the most confusing in the area of finance. In addition to meaning "money financing the business", which appears on the liabilities side of the balance sheet, capital also refers to assets: a **capital asset** is an asset which will be categorised as a fixed asset in the balance sheet.

Capital spend refers to spending on items which go into the balance sheet as fixed assets, which means that they will remain in the business for more than one year. It is not spending which simply reduces profit. Spending which is charged against profit in the profit and loss account "**expensed**", the opposite of capital spend, is called **revenue spend**).

Because of the sums of money involved, capital spending has a major impact on cash planning. If an item is included in a capital spend programme, in the capital spend budget or forecast, then, assuming there is enough money to pay for it, it is very important that the spend is completed on time. There is a practical problem here: it is in the nature of business difficult to find the time to complete a major purchase and the purchase is often subject to delay. However, if a project slips off the end of the current planning period, it may need to be reapproved. This may be difficult, especially if the financial climate changes.

Capital spend decisions

The decision process concerning whether or not to spend money on expensive fixed assets – capital spend projects – is called "**capital spend appraisal**". This can be another major contribution of the finance function.

When a large spend decision is being considered, the company must take into account that the benefits of the investment may not happen immediately and may continue to happen well into the future. The problem with this is that if a benefit is not received until, say, Year 3 of the project, the value of the benefit, in today's value is less than if the benefit is received today. This is not only about inflation – the value reduces over time even if inflation is zero.

Let me explain this simply: if I borrow £100 from you and then say to you I can either give you the £100 back next month, or, in three years' time, you will choose £100 next month. There are two reasons why you would prefer your £100 immediately:

- It avoids the risk that I won't repay you.

- You can take the £100 and immediately invest it (for example in a bank, or a project).

However, if I say that I will give you £130 in three years' time, you may be unsure as to which option is best – to take £100 in a month or £130 in three years' time. (In economic terms you could be said to be '**indifferent**'.)

Companies need to take into account the **time value of money** when appraising capital spend decisions. In order to do this, they use a technique called **Discounted Cash Flow (DCF)**. DCF applies a discount factor to reduce the value of cash inflows, which will occur in the future and will result from capital spend decisions, to today's value. The discount factor which a company uses is called the **'hurdle rate'**. The positive and negative result from all the cash inflows and outflows, discounted to today's value, is called the "**net present value (NPV)**".

It's also possible to calculate the hurdle rate required to discount the net present value of a capital project to zero. This rate is called the "**internal rate of return (IRR)**".

Here's an example of a capital spend decision:

Let's take the following simple assumptions:

	£
Immediate capital spend (new machinery)	3000
Increased sales (begin after 1 year for 4 years)	2000
Increased costs associated with sales	1000
Hurdle rate	10%

The hurdle rate of 10% (=0.1) is applied to the annual cash flows in the following way:

Year One:
$$\frac{1000}{(1 + 0.1)} = 909$$

Year Two:
$$\frac{1000}{(1 + 0.1) \times (1 + 0.1)} = 826$$

Year Three:
$$\frac{1000}{(1 + 0.1) \times (1 + 0.1) \times (1 + 0.1)} = 751$$

This would give the following position.

Figure 2.15 Capital investment appraisal

	Year				
	0	**1**	**2**	**3**	**4**
	£	£	£	£	£
Start up cost	-3000				
Sales		2000	2000	2000	2000
Cost of sales		-1000	-1000	-1000	-1000
Net cash effect	**-3000**	**1000**	**1000**	**1000**	**1000**
Discounted Cash Flow (at 10%)	-3000	909	826	751	683
NPV (at 10%) =	**169**				
Discounted Cash Flow (at 12.6%)	-3000	888	789	700	623
NPV (at 12.6%)	**0**		**Project IRR = 12.6%**		

The cash inflow in year one has been discounted at 10%.

If we now add the value of the discounted cash outflows and compare this with the immediate investment in year 0, we get a difference of +169 . This means that at 10% hurdle rate the project gives a result or "net present value" of +169.

The hurdle rate required to bring net present value of this project to zero is 12.6%. This means the internal rate of return is 12.6%.

Internal rate of return is one of the key, and most common, higher level finance concepts with regard to investment decisions. In addition to being used to evaluate internal spend projects it is also used by external investors when considering whether or not to supply equity capital to companies.

The whole area of Discounted Cash Flow generates enormous confusion. Some senior executives never really understand it! However, it's not so difficult to understand, and it's worth taking time to understand because of its importance and very frequent usage (also, if you can explain it, you'll appear to be brilliant!).

Payroll

Payroll is the name normally given to the department responsible for paying the workforce of the company. It sometimes sits in the HR function, but more commonly sits in the finance function. The reason for this is to provide a split of responsibility between managing the workforce records and paying of the workforce. If these operations sit in the same function, there is an increased risk of payment fraudulently being made to an employee who does not exist.

Internal audit

Internal audit is the name given to the department which performs internal checks to ensure that the company is conforming to internal financial policies and procedures. The issue of whether the company is conforming or not to policies and procedures, and rules and regulations, whether internal or external, is called "compliance". The process of checking and reporting is the responsibility of the Internal Audit Manager, sometimes called the "Compliance Manager".

Although internal auditors perform an inspection role, they should not be viewed negatively and can be extremely useful to executives in two ways:

- they can make recommendations as to working practices, the implementation of which often eliminates problems and reduces anxiety.

- where compliance is in place, they will report it, to the benefit of the complying executive.

Internal audit does not always sit in the finance function. Sometimes, to avoid the situation where finance is inspecting itself, it reports direct to the Managing Director/CEO.

Operations

"**Operations**" refers either to producing goods or providing services. More generally, operations can refer to anything which the company does, but with emphasis on those things which either directly or indirectly satisfy the customer. "Operations" could therefore be broadened to include research and development, design and distribution.

Production operations

Production involves input, process and output of material. If the material physically moves through the process, this is called "**throughput**". The change which is made to the material during the production process is called "**conversion**". The conversion may involve applying labour or adding materials. The labour and materials involved in the input and conversion of the production process are classified as direct elements of production and are therefore direct costs – "direct labour" and "direct materials". There are three types of materials connected to the production process:

- **raw materials** – materials which are completely unprocessed, (that is, to which no conversion has been applied).

- **work in progress** – sometimes called "**work in process**" – materials which are part processed (to which some conversion has been applied).

- **finished goods** – the output from the production process conversion (where the conversion is complete).

There are other cost elements which are required for the production to take place: these typically include space, equipment, training costs, and energy costs. Although these costs may not vary with the level of production, they are directly connected to the production process and are therefore normally called "direct costs".

So, a very simple production model, illustrated in Figure 2.16, looks like this:

Figure 2.16 Simple production model

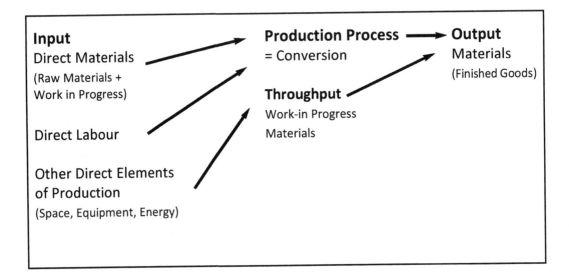

As the production process continues, financially two things happen at the same time. Cost, either direct or indirect, is **incurred**, and value is added to the item being produced.

Because physical goods are required to be ready for a physical production process, either in the form of raw materials, work in progress, or fixed goods, the typical production process involves keeping **stocks**, also called **inventory**, of these items at the various stages of production.

? *Why does the company need stock?*

Stock of materials is required to enable the production process to continue where the supply of materials does not exactly match the amount required by the next stage of business operations. If the next stage of operations is production, then the required stock will be of raw materials or work in progress. If the next stage is transportation to the customer, then it will be of finished goods.

? Why is keeping stock a cost to the company?

Keeping stock is a cost to the company for the following reasons:

- it occupies space and needs to be managed.

- it can go bad or be spoilt (especially in the case of fresh foods).

- it represents a money value to the company which could be used elsewhere if stocks were lower (we say it 'ties up' cash).

Minimisation of stock is a key target of the Operations Director. It's an important way in which to be competitive on costs, and therefore on price.

Service operations

A service operation, for example, banking or consultancy, differs from a production operation in the following important ways:

- the service is performed immediately – there is no time delay between the providing of the service, the incurring of the costs, and the adding of value. This means that a service error is immediately visible to the customer, and that the company's quality is immediately affected. Production problems can often be put right, and, even if they cannot, the customer need not be aware of the problem.

- the providing of the service often involves, and is affected by, the customer (for example the service provided by a driving instructor very largely depends on the aptitude and the attitude of the customer)

- the personal qualities and behaviour of the person providing the service is of high importance (at its most basic, most people would prefer to be served by a pretty girl with an attractive smile: a fact which gives the pretty girl a competitive advantage)

Typically, service operations involve the usage of materials during the performance of the service. This may or may not involve making improvements to a physical product belonging to a customer. However, as nothing is produced, there is no involvement of, and therefore no stock of, raw materials or work-in-progress. Only spare parts, finished goods or indirect materials are used and therefore require stock levels.

The Operations Director's challenge

Any work activity, and therefore any business activity, involves optimising the relationship between input and output. Input, whether labour (= time), or material, space, or equipment, is referred to as "**resources**". The more resources are used, the higher the costs that are incurred. The task of any manager is to optimise the efficient use of resources, which means optimising the relationship between cost and value added through his processes.

Input required, either for production or providing a service, not only costs money but is in limited supply. Of course, money is itself limited, but even if the company is "cash rich", labour, materials, space and equipment are always in limited supply. If something is in limited supply, and this can become an issue for the company, we call it a "**constraint**". Of course, as the Operations Director attempts to reduce costs, for example by reducing stock levels, direct labour or space, the availability of the resources decreases, and the constraint becomes more severe. He must therefore maximise efficiency, that is the balance between input and output, or cost and added value, within the constraints imposed on him and which he imposes on himself. However, he must ensure that resources are not so sparingly managed that production has to stop, or slow down, or that the service is affected.

The Operations Director's challenge is a severe one – mistakes and problems in production are potentially extremely costly because:

- the cost of resources is especially high.

- problems and mistakes can be expensive to put right.

- there is potential to lose relatively large amounts of revenue and cash flow because the production output is the basis of what the company is selling.

- customer service, and therefore customer relations may be seriously affected by production problems (for example delivery may be late). Lost customers are difficult to replace!

(?) How can efficiency be maximised in operations?

Normally the efficiency of production will increase or, put another way, the cost of production relative to output and value added will decrease, according to the scale of production. Normally, the more a company produces the more "cost efficient" it becomes. This is because some costs vary with the level of production ("variable costs"), but some costs remain the same ("fixed costs"). As the level of production rises (of course up to a limit), fixed costs are divided by an increased number of production units, so that while total cost increases, total cost per unit decreases. On the other hand, if production stops, direct costs will also stop, but fixed costs remain the same and are now divided into less units – fixed costs per unit increases and therefore total cost per unit also increases. Stoppages and equipment changeovers are expensive!

The economic advantage where cost efficiency is increased by an increase in production volume is called "**economies of scale**".

In addition to production volume increase, production cost efficiency is typically maximised by the following:

- adequate inventory levels;

- a constant and small variety of product (meaning long production runs, low set up and change over costs, and low costs of management input time);

- infrequent changes in production, location and space utilisation;

- sufficient capital investment in good quality equipment;

- a stable level of production;

- an achievable level of quality standards applied (more on this later);

- good systems.

The Operations Manager has to balance his requirement of maximising cost efficiency with satisfying the requirements of other company functions. Sales and marketing, for example, may demand a wide product variety and frequent changes to products.

 What are the main production methods?

There are three main production methods:

- **line** – where a product moves along the production line as work is done to it; examples are a bottling plant and vehicle assembly.

- **job** – where one product only is produced at a time (a "**job lot**" is where a small number of one type of product is produced at a time). Examples of job production might be hand-crafted furniture or very high quality cars.

- **batch – w**here a specific and limited number of similar products are made in one production run. Examples may be magazines, or textile products like curtains.

Generally, the methods of production have the following features:

Line:

- high capital investment and set up costs;
- long production runs;
- goods produced go into stock;

Batch/job:

- low capital investment and set up costs;
- short production runs;
- goods produced not for stock but to order;
- typically higher specification goods, tailor-made for customer.

How does the operations function connect to other company functions?

For the operations function to be effective, there must be a strong contact, or 'interface', with other functions in the company.

Production and finance

One way in which the finance function can help the operations function is by setting a cost target, either a budget or a forecast, for the production or service processes, and for the products to be made. It can also help by analysing the costs into fixed costs and variable costs. This type of costing is called "marginal costing".

What's the purpose of marginal costing?

Splitting costs into fixed and variable can help production, and the company in general, in two main ways:

- It can be used to calculate the "**breakeven point**" for a particular product. The breakeven point is the amount of units which are required to be produced in order to stop making a loss on the product and start making a profit. Let's take an example as Figure 2.17 overleaf.

Figure 2.17 Breakeven point calculation

A company sells a product for £30 a unit. It has the following "cost structure":

- variable costs £10 per unit;
- fixed costs £1000.

In this case, if the company sells nothing at all it loses £1000. The situation is improved by £20 for every unit the company sells. Therefore fixed costs are completely compensated for, or equalled, when 50 units are sold (see equation below). We say that every unit makes a "contribution" of £20 per unit. Breakeven is the point at which fixed costs are equal to the contribution from sales. The formula for calculating the breakeven point is simply:

> Fixed costs
> Contribution per unit

> In this case:

> 1,000   = 50
> 20

If the company sells produces and sells 49, it will make a loss of 20. If it produces and sells 51, it will make a profit of 20.

- it can help a company to decide whether it is more profitable to stop producing a particular product which might appear to be unprofitable. Figure 2.18 takes another situation.

Figure 2.18 Retaining vs removing an unprofitable product line

A company produces two products, product A and product B. It shows the following result:

	A	B
Sales Units	50,000	100,000
	£	£
Sales Revenue	100,000	100,000
Variable Costs	(50,000)	(75,000)
Gross Profit	50,000	25,000
Fixed Costs (based on units)	(20,000)	40,000)
Net Profit	30,000	(15,000)

On the face of it, Product B is unprofitable. It only makes a gross profit of £25,000 on 100,000 units. Fixed costs are allocated on the basis of units (at £0.40 per unit) and so for Product B are £40,000, resulting in a loss for Product B of £15,000. However, if we removed product B altogether and produced only product A in the same quantity the company would make a loss of 10,000. This is £25,000 worse than the combined result including product B. The reason for this is that the gross product of product B, or the **contribution** to fixed cost, is lost.

Production and research and development/marketing/design

We've seen that one of the strongest challenges faced by businesses is the way that markets and the environment are constantly changing. One of the key functions in the company's response to change is research and development. Once the company understands the requirements of the market, research and development will drive the company's ability to convert these requirements into production. We have already seen that operations should only produce or provide those products required by marketing. The objective of research and development is the introduction of new products and production processes. Normally, this is very strongly driven by marketing, and not by operations. Product design, whilst attempting to satisfy the demands of cheap and efficient production, must also point mainly towards the marketing function, and therefore to the requirements of the customer, not the Operations Director.

"Just in time" production

One of the key balances which the Operations Director must strike is between that of having sufficient inventory, so that production is not disrupted, and keeping inventory, and its carrying costs, to a minimum. **"Just in time"** is a strategy used by Operations for managing work-in-progress stock levels. Very simply, a "Just in time" production method tells operations exactly when a part is required by production, at the next stage of production, or from production, thereby minimising stock levels and their carrying costs.

Production and sales/planning/IT

A strong connection between sales, planning and operations will help to reduce inventory levels (stock levels). There may be a conflict between requests from sales, for a varied product offer, and from operations for a simplified product offer. An IT (**Information Technology**) system which frequently connects the three areas in respect of the control of stock levels is called a **Materials Requirement Planning (MRP)** system.

MRP is a complex area but there are basically three forecast inputs into the MRP system:

- The materials requirement 'pulled' into production from the sales forecast.

- The forecast of materials required to produce the individual product (normally 'exploded' on the document called the Bill of Materials).

- The levels of stock of materials which already exist, or the forecast of future stock levels, required for the production process.

Supply chain management

In the supermarket business, where there is no production process, the operational efficiency is optimised by moving materials as quickly as possible to replenish those lost when a sale is made. The materials are "pulled" by the system from the supplier, through the distribution centres, to the point of sale (the supermarket shelves). The objective is to minimise the stock levels everywhere in the organisation.

It's very interesting to visit a large supermarket distribution centre. There's constant movement because it's not a storage facility. The problem of holding quantities of stock is passed by the supermarket to the supplier, who accepts this as a price to be paid for the enormous volumes of product which the supermarket orders. The whole area of management of this movement of goods from the supplier through distribution centres to the customer base is called **"supply chain management"**.

Logistics efficiency in service operations

Efficiency in service operations is generally maximised by:

- a stable level of demand for the service, or the ability of the company to respond quickly and with minimum additional cost to "peak times";

- sufficient availability of suitable, trained staff;

- good systems;

- availability of parts.

When all this is in place, response to the needs of the customer can be quick and effective. If any one of these things is missing, service can fall over.

Where spare parts are required by service operations, the function of logistics is about getting the **right part** to the **right place** at the **right time** at the **right cost**.

The part is pulled by the system from the service performed with the customer.

Availability of parts is key. I recently had a problem with my cooker hob (I really am not good with gadgets). After two visits to my home (involving me taking time off work), and a delay of eleven winter weeks, the part was delivered to the company but was found to be damaged in transit. At the next visit to my home (more time off work) the engineer discovered that the box contained an incorrect part. The result? They cut me a deal, at further cost to the company.

Operations and people

We saw earlier how important it is for an organisation to have happy staff. In addition to avoiding the problems of staff turnover, absenteeism and timekeeping, happy staff in the production function often mean a better quality of product.

In service operations which involve personal contact, the quality of service cannot be separated from the individual providing the service (of which more later).

In the area of production there are a number of factors which are now accepted as leading to job satisfaction in production workers:

- **team working**, where experience shows that workers working in teams can identify with a larger task and assume more responsibility for quality and efficiency. One of the classic examples of team working in manufacturing is the car manufacturer, Volvo.

- **job rotation**, where workers move from one job to another in the same production function.

- **good conditions**, including work space, lighting, air quality, regular breaks and refreshment facilities.

It's easy to forget how far we have come with this. In the first company I started work in, in the early 70s, the workers ate their lunch by the machines, or outside on the floor of the yard in nice weather. Taking a break meant going to the toilet for a smoke.

- **fair pay for unpleasant work** ('dirty money') or inconvenient work (e.g. shift allowances).

- **ergonomic factors** (expert positioning and arrangement of machines, seats etc. to optimise health and comfort).

Of course, these things have all been hard won over many years. In the early days of production society provided no security, job markets were much less developed, work alternatives were restricted and therefore workers were exploited. Pay and conditions have improved as a result of **collective bargaining** and now have the force of the law.

Today, although companies still continually struggle to find a balance between profit and industrial harmony, they are conscious that workers are less desperate for work and are more mobile between labour markets. Companies need to measure up to competing standards and provide satisfactory conditions as a matter of course.

Quality

I've already mentioned that "**quality**" is a key business word. The *Compact Oxford English Dictionary* defines quality as: "a degree of excellence of something as measured against other similar things". So, quality is relative: you can only say "it's a quality car" if you have some idea of how good or bad cars generally are.

A company's quality, culminating in the quality of its products offered for sale, is a key factor in its success. There are clear reasons for this:

- modern markets and customers are extremely quality conscious: any poor quality product is likely to fail over more than the very short-term.

- the cost of putting right quality problems is very high.

- it takes time after the quality problems are fixed for the quality of the product to be perceived as satisfactory and for demand for the product to be restored.

An example of a poor quality image not going away it that of the British car manufacturer, Rover. In the 1970s Rover, part of the UK car manufacturer British Leyland, suffered from problems of build quality and reliability, partly due to industrial relations problems. The problem contributed to the company's financial difficulties. In 1979, the company joined forces with the Japanese manufacturer Honda. Despite producing good quality cars after that, the public perception of Rover as having quality problems lasted throughout the '80s.

As I've been writing this, Toyota have recalled millions of cars due to concerns about the braking systems or sticking accelerator pedals. The problems have resulted in expensive suspension to production. The long-term damage to the Toyota brand will take months to assess.

According to British Quality Standards, "quality" is defined as "the totality of features and characteristics of a product or service that bear on its ability to satisfy a given need". The simple phrase I remember from my MBA course is "**fitness for purpose**".

Quality is sometimes divided into:

- **Functional quality**, which broadly refers to whether, and how well, a product performs its designed function.

- **Non-functional quality**, broadly meaning how good quality a product (or service) is, or is perceived to be, for reasons other than what it is specifically designed to do (or provide).

Let's look at these two quality concepts in a bit more detail:

Functional quality
Functional quality can consist of different elements:

- Whether or not the product or service simply does or does not do what it was designed to do. One example would be: whether or not a pencil eraser erases pencil marks (have you noticed how many don't?).

     Taking a rather different example, the phrase "not fit for purpose" was used by the UK Home Secretary, John Reid, when describing the Home

Office Immigration Directorate in 2006. It was, he said, inadequate in terms of its scope, IT, leadership, management, and processes.

- How long the product continues to perform the function that it was designed to perform. This could be how long it lasts (for example, in the case of a pair of trousers, without wearing out (the "**durability**") or, in the case of a vacuum cleaner, how long it works without it breaking down ("the **reliability**"). The technical term for a product ceasing to function is "**failure**".

- The extent to which the product or service is satisfactory, when performing its designed function, for the user. (An example of this would be if a chair is durable and can be sat on, but is not comfortable for the seated person, then it could hardly be described as a "quality chair".)

Non-functional quality
Non-functional quality could be described as a combination of two things:

- "**intrinsic quality**", which concerns how good a thing really is. Intrinsic quality is additional to functionality; it is often about feel (texture of clothing or food) or appearance (style, design and absence of defects in a piece of furniture or an electrical product).

- "**perceived quality**" concerns how good the customer feels when actually using the product – how good it *seems* to be. The product may affect the customer's self-image in a positive or negative way. If you were to spend £2,000 on an Armani suit you would need to know not only that it has functional quality (that is comfortable, keeps you warm and will last more than three months), and intrinsic quality (that it was free from fabric defect, was beautiful to the touch, and looked stylish), but you would also want it to make you feel good because of the brand name and image(perceived quality). Clearly the self-image aspect of perceived quality is strongly driven by marketing activity in building and advertising brands.

Case Study

Building consumer interest through perceived quality is a key essential in advertising and has been used to sell quite simple products.

A classic UK marketing success story is the Yorkie Bar, now manufactured by Nestle, but originally manufactured by Rowntrees of York. In fact, the business reality was a supply of cheap cocoa, a perceived gap in the market, and a resulting simple milk chocolate bar. The perceived quality of the product was that it was "manly" (befitting the image of the north of England) – it was ostensibly aimed at men, and was supported by television ads featuring sexy truck drivers, with the controversial tag line "It's not for girls". A billboard on York railway station had the slogan "Welcome to York, where the men are hunky and the chocolate's chunky".

I have also mentioned the Hovis TV ad for bread (in fact the advert has been voted Britain's most popular TV ad of all time). The ad, which features a boy on a bike, is set in the past and filmed on a beautiful historic street. It features music by Dvorak and was directed by Ridley Scott. The ad promotes a perceived quality connected to a sense of traditional British goodness.

Quality and the company

Product or service quality very much depends on the quality of the company supplying the product or providing the service. Quality in an organisation consists of two further aspects:

- **Quality Assurance (QA)** – the resource inputs, procedures and processes which determine whether the product can be produced or the service provided in accordance with the required quality targets.

- **Quality Control (QC)** – the extent to which the company's quality targets are achieved, and the procedures and processes which are used to test or check this.

The terms are used interchangeably but, in general, **quality management** consists of quality assurance and quality control, and it leads to product quality.

We've already identified an important feature of business organisations in general – that they are interrelated; one part affects another. This is particularly so in the case of quality. A company's product quality depends on a company's processes, and both of these depend on the setting up and achieving of quality targets.

A company must have good quality everywhere, not only in little pockets that are directly connected to the production or to the service process. Quality cannot not be 'inspected in' to the product or service and it cannot be packed in as the final stage of production. "**Total Quality Management (TQM)**" expresses the idea of quality *pervading* the company and being driven from the top of the company. So the quality equation is :

Figure 2.19 The quality equation

TOTAL QUALITY ASSURANCE + TOTAL QUALITY CONTROL

=

TOTAL QUALITY MANAGEMENT

=

TOTAL PRODUCT QUALITY

 So what is product quality about?

Basically, the objective of quality assurance and quality control in production is to create a finished product with the minimum of defects and faults.

- A **defect** is an inadequacy which causes something to be less than perfect. A defect may be in a process or a finished product and may be caused by defective input material. Very often a defect in a finished product is visual: for example, a blemish on a shirt.

- A **fault** is an imperfection in the operation or performance of the product. Examples could be a light which flickers or a sound system which produces distorted music. Defects in input materials or processes may cause faults in the finished product.

How are defects and faults identified?

Inspection is a major tool in quality control. Inspection does not create quality. It works if there is a target, sometimes called an **"Acceptable Quality Level" (AQL)**, and sometimes a **"benchmark"**, in respect of the achieved level of lack of defects and faults in production output. Of course, the ideal situation is zero defects and faults, but in practice this is impossible and the company has another balance to strike: it must balance its AQL against its cost targets.

It's also normally impossible to inspect everything so a company operates a **sampling** policy. If the sample inspection indicates an AQL, then the finished job, product or unit is allowed to progress to dispatch or the point of sale (in respect of the finished product) or to the next stage of production (in the case of work-in-progress).

If the sample inspected indicates a quality deficiency against the AQL or benchmark then, assuming it is cost effective to do so, the material or product may be **reworked**, which means the production process may be repeated or part-repeated. If the material or product cannot be reworked, then the affected product will have to be scrapped, or possibly sold as defective, or **"seconds"**. One of the problems with sampling is that it may involve spoiling the product inspected to some extent. In this case, it is known as **"destructive sampling"**. If the sample inspected indicates a serious endemic problem, then the company is faced with the prospect of making a significant change to the process. This is known as **"business process reengineering"**.

Service quality
Management of quality in a service operation presents an additional set of challenges.

How do you manage service quality?

The measurement of service quality depends, of course, on the service being offered. It may be possible for the person performing the service to record his achievement – customers visited, installations completed, customer problems solved etc. Of course recording actual performance is only of value where the information is accurate, or **verifiable**, and if there are specific targets in place to indicate the required service level. In other cases, it can be more difficult – how do you measure a bank assistant's handling of an unsatisfied customer who won't go away? How do you respond to customers who say they can never get through by phone, when every time you try, as manager, it immediately works? Measurement in these cases is problematic because:

- The measurement system is too difficult to implement.

- Even if it is implemented and proves that the quality of service is good, it may not improve the customer's perception (remember Rover).

How can a company deliver quality service?

In general, there are three technical building blocks of good quality service:

- required parts available on time;

- user friendly, efficient computer systems;

- available personnel;

Where service operations rely on personal contact with the customer, the people management factors discussed earlier become vital:

- good training (in dealing with customers);

- motivated staff (in service operations in particular this also results from cross- functional support from throughout the company);

- empowered staff with correct information and authority (even in a restaurant, it makes a significant difference to the "service act" if a waiter or waitress knows that it's possible to have mashed potato instead of chips!);

Where service involves personal customer contact, quality becomes increasingly "non- functional". The effectiveness of the service will be very significantly influenced by the customer's perception. Of course, speed and efficiency are extremely important, but how the customer feels about the service provided is also critical. If you have to use a vehicle breakdown service, the service you receive will be of higher value to you if the patrolman is friendly and sympathetic.

If he's cold, disinterested or impolite, then the service, even though efficiently provided, will be of less value.

Certainly, in the UK, and I say this after many years of both receiving and providing service, customers will forgive a surprising amount of technical service shortfalls if they like the person they are dealing with. Even when working in the gas business, when customers were without heating, I received this type of comment: "I'm not so bothered about the heating – I just wanted somebody to talk to." Personally, I like going into Barclays Bank, even if I have to queue and they charge me for my account, because I like the people.

Continuous improvement

The concept of total quality management has strong roots in Japanese manufacturing, in particular in the automobile manufacturing industry. Specifically, the Japanese were responsible for introducing **continuous improvement**. The Japanese word for improvement, "**Kaizen**", is often used. A "continuous improvement process" (CIP or CI) is defined by Wikipedia as an "ongoing effort to improve products, services or processes".(9) This effort seeks to obtain "incremental' improvement" over time, rather than a "breakthrough" improvement all at once. In a continuous improvement process the company's operational processes are constantly evaluated and improved in the light of their efficiency, and effectiveness. "Kaizen" is particularly associated with the Japanese car manufacturer Toyota, despite their recent issues, where all workers on the line are expected to stop production if any problem is discovered and, along with their supervisor, suggest improvements to the manufacturing process.

One method the Japanese have introduced in order to achieve continuous improvement is "**quality circles**". These are small groups of employees, possibly between four and eight in number, who represent different functions of the company, and different parts of the operations process. The role of a quality circle is simple: to identify and analyse quality issues, to suggest process improvements and, afterwards, approval by management, to implement process improvements.

Quality circles are an example of the interactive nature of business. They surely work better in an environment where management style is participative in nature, and in turn promotes a participative working environment. Quality circles are not likely to be effective if communication is "top down" and the culture dictatorial.

Part 3

Practical Aspects of Business

Starting a Business

One of the most frequently asked questions in my classes is:

(?) *What's involved in starting a business?*

One of the only ways of making serious money is to own your own business. However, let me also give you a word of caution: according to Patricia Schaefer in her internet article *The Seven Pitfalls of Business Failure*:

"The latest statistics from the Small Business Administration (SBA) show that 'two-thirds of new employer establishments survive at least two years, and 44 percent survive at least four years.' This is a far cry from the previous long-held belief that 50 percent of businesses fail in the first year and 95 percent fail within five years".(10)

OK, but this means that statistically your new business is **likely to fail**, with attendant financial loss and heartache. In the words of the novelist Graham Greene, said through the mouth of a retired bank employee, "Whims (fanciful ideas) so often end in bankruptcy" (11). Have you noticed how often a retail outlet or restaurant or bar opens up, only to change hands again within a couple of years? The average person finds starting a new business a hard road to travel down.

So, again, what IS involved in starting a business?

An Idea

First, you need a good idea, something which not only seems to have commercial logic but which interests you and fires you up. Go for an idea which can be converted into an excellent product or service of which you can be proud.

If the idea is for a product or service which is tried and tested, and for which you perceive a gap exists in the market (e.g. an Italian restaurant in an area where one doesn't exist), then it is likely to be less risky. If the idea is for a product or service for which the market is already well served, then it will help to have a **unique selling proposition** – something which makes your product more attractive than the competitors'.

If the idea is for a product or service which is completely new – an innovation – then the potential risk increases because nothing is established: the demand for the product and the methods of production, distribution and selling will all be unclear.

Research

Next, you need to **research** your idea. Bounce it off people who've been around a bit and won't hang back from giving you hard messages and advice. There are many, many experienced people in the UK who, for one reason or another, are not doing a lot. The internet is a very useful source of information. There are also organisations which may help, for example "Business Link". Try to talk to people selectively who work in a similar area or who may have tried something similar. Talk to successful people. Don't be afraid of aiming high. If approached correctly, successful people are often incredibly helpful. If you talk to unsuccessful people, the comments you get are likely to be negative and worth little.

A team

If your idea survives examination by yourself and others, the next requirement is to consider who will be your people. In my experience even well-established businesses make ambitious plans without considering who will actually make things happen. Of course, you can recruit, but there are basic problems here:

- the people you recruit will be new to the idea and unknown – there are a lot of well-presented but not particularly useful people about.

- recruitment is time-consuming.

- you will need to pay the people you employ immediately.

It would be ideal to gather a few selected friends, colleagues or business partners who would be prepared to back the project without pay, or with minimum pay. You're going to need strong, positive, trustworthy and cheap people. Who could that be? Well, for example, a friend, or a friend of a friend who is not working full time, a retired older person who has plenty of time and cash, or a young person with a rich father!

Some money
Of course, most new businesses need **start-up finance**, called capital and some-times called **seed money**. There are two ways to raise business capital: you can borrow it, which is called debt capital, or you can get people to invest in your busi-ness, which is called equity capital. There are issues connected with both of these. If you try to borrow, the possible problems are that:

- it will be difficult because the business is not established and you have no reputation.

- you may not have any **security (collateral)** to offer to cover the eventuality that the business cannot repay the loan.

- the business may not generate cash immediately with which to pay back or service (pay the interest on) the loan.

If you try to get somebody to invest in your business, the possible problems are that:

- the investor is likely to want to control your business.

- they will want an **exit** (get out) from the arrangement as soon as possible because they will not want their money to be at risk for any length of time. As a result they are unlikely to back long-term plans or investment.

A business plan
In order to raise finance you'll need a business plan. This needs to include the whole concept of your new business, from the idea to the practicalities of putting

the idea into operation and sustaining the business into the future.

You can get good advice on how to construct a business plan, and on starting a business in general, from the internet.

A good way to approach writing a business plan is to think about the audience and the questions in their mind. Whether it's a bank, a venture capitalist, a small investor (found through for example a UK Business Link contact), some friends, or your father-in-law, they will want to know the answer to the following questions:

Question 1:
Is the business going to fail?

The main reasons why businesses fail are:

- the product simply doesn't sell.

- even if the product does sell, the business runs out of cash. This can result from the fact that credit may be difficult to negotiate, and suppliers want quick or immediate payment. So, again, don't be afraid of aiming high in terms of the amount of cash requested. Many businesses fail because insufficient cash was put into the business at the start.

- a competitor's action destroys the business.

- the business proves to be too difficult to manage or the original business model is incorrect. This results in the management team losing motivation and leaving the business or the business running out of control and ultimately failing.

Question 2 is:
Who makes up the team which will run the business?
Are they experienced? Are they strong, motivated, persuasive and competent? In particular, is there a competent person to look after the finances?

Question 3 is:
How much cash is the business going to generate? How soon? For how long?

Remember, it's cash flow that banks and investors will look for, not profit, so profit figures need to be adjusted for "non cash" charges to profit. Banks need to be sure that the loan and interest can be repaid in a relatively short timeframe and investors not only want a quick exit but a healthy return on their investment (remember IRR?). They will set a demanding hurdle rate to assess the potential cash returns.

Finally, a wise and kindly family member may ask the following realistic question:

? *Are you really right for this venture or are you (and your partner?) going to become tired, stressed and miserable?*

As we say in business, this is not "rocket science", but the business plan does need to be laid out correctly. You need to state clearly: what the business is, how it will work, who will run it and how much money (in the form not only of profit but of **cash**) it will make. In formal terms, the plan needs to be an outline of:

- the market and its competitors (it's a good idea to mention any specific sources of information);

- your marketing approach;

- your total operations (sourcing, storing and distributing the product);

- your team and their strengths

- your financial projections.

The business plan needs to be "fronted" up with a summary of the whole business proposition, called an "**Executive Summary**". It should not just be the idea for the product.

Finally, good presentation is vital: any detailed papers in the business plan, for example the cash flow forecast or complicated diagrams explaining the operation, should be included at the end, not in the body of the plan. Take care over typing it, or get it professionally typed, and put a nice cover on it.

One final practicality: it's worth investigating, carefully, whether or not you need to form a limited company and whether, if you do, you need the services of a financial advisor. The potential advantages of a limited company are that:

- it may reduce the tax bill;

- it could protect against possible liability;

- it looks official.

However, limited companies do involve work, or expense, in completing the required forms: you would need to submit externally audited financial statements and other documents. This is a pain – I know, I've done it (I recently received a notice saying I owed £900 in respect of an employee return which I had not returned, when my company had no employees!)

However, to repeat: don't let me put you off!

Business Strategy

Let's, once again, start at "square one".

 ## *What is strategy?*

Strategy, from the Greek work "stratos" which means "army". **Strategy** is about major decisions and overall direction. The *BNET* business dictionary definition of strategy is:

"a planned course of action undertaken to achieve the goals and objectives of an organization". (12)

So a **strategy** is about the **long-term** and it's about **overall objectives**. It's about the "big picture". It is *not* the same as "**tactics**". To use a military analogy, strategy is about whether or not to fight a battle; tactics is about how to fight it.

Let's have a look at some typical strategic decisions:

Increase the size of the company
The process of increasing the size of the company, or the scale of its operations, is called "**expansion**". Companies typical decide to expand operations for the following reasons:

- **cost efficiency.** As operations increase, fixed costs can be spread more thinly, which means they can be divided amongst proportionately more output. The increased cost efficiency achieved by expanding operations is "economies of scale".

- **profit increase.** Cost efficiency is about increasing **profitability**. Sometimes, however, companies increase operations simply to increase the amount of profit. Especially when companies are cash rich, the directors may decide that investing cash into increased operations will generate more profit for the shareholders than investing the cash in a bank or on the money markets.

At the start of the 1990s Tesco, the UK supermarket giant, was a market leader in the UK supermarket business, had around 100,000 employees and made enormous profits. Despite this, they made a strategic decision to expand overseas. Why? Because, with the company being cash rich and the UK market saturated, the directors clearly decided that the shareholders could be better rewarded by the increase in profit which would result from expansion overseas than by remaining only in the UK.

- **critical mass** – this is where expansion concerns achieving a level of strength in the market place, at which the company can control suppliers, logistics arrangements or markets. The company may need a larger scale of operations simply to achieve brand recognition. Alternatively, it may need increased size to justify further specific strategic decisions and the accompanying investment.

Decrease the scale of a company's operations
The opposite of "expansion" is "**contraction**". Companies decide to contract for two main reasons:

- the available market diminishes.

- the company needs to make cost savings.

Very often a company will use contraction as an opportunity to remove inefficient people and processes. This is called "**streamlining**". The Compact Oxford English Dictionary definition of "streamline" is: *"make more efficient by employing faster or similar working methods"*. Streamlining may involve reducing people (also called "**downsizing**") and making the remaining people cover more areas of operation. It may also involve reducing the bureaucracy in terms of levels of people, or complexity of processes or paperwork. So, streamlining is generally about achieving less, with proportionately less people and administrative systems, or the same, with less people and administrative systems. If a company decides to pull out of a market or operation, or to terminate one of its products, the word "rationalisation" can be used.

Move into new markets

A company may decide to move into a new market with its existing product range. It may do this through the use of targeted advertising campaigns or by entering a new geographical area, for example an overseas market as in the case of Tesco.

A company may decide to offer completely new and different products or services. This is known as product "**diversification**" and can reduce the risk factor involved in a company's products being too limited. A company can diversify by brandstretching, which is using a well known brand to offer a completely new product or service (remember supermarkets selling financial services?).

Move geographically

Companies may decide to locate a new operation in a different part of the country, or in an overseas country. This decision is normally about cost (especially cheap labour and land) but it may also be about locating the operation close to the market for the goods to be sold, or close to a labour market. Where a company decides to move to a new location this is called "relocation". Where a company decides to expand so as to achieve a worldwide presence, this is known as "**globalisation**".

Change operation in the same market

The company may decide to reposition its product within an existing market by increasing or decreasing the price (that is to say, by moving "upmarket" or "downmarket"). A company may also remain in the same market with the same basic product positioning, but decide to attack the market in a specific way, for example with selectively larger price discounts than those offered by competitors.

An example of a pricing strategy, apparently not connected to the decision to move the product up or down the market, is in the computer printer business. The decision has clearly been made that the main revenue generation in respect of computer printers is not from the sale of the printer itself but from the sale of the cartridge (a colour cartridge retails for little short of the cost of a printer). Supplies for computers are called "**consumables**", and the sale of consumables can generate enormous revenue relative to the sale of the hardware. There are numerous examples in other industries where sales of accessories, or spare parts, create more revenue than sales of the finished product.

Change product or market

Companies formulate strategy as a result of the actions, or potential actions, of other organisations which have an impact, or potential impact, on the company's operations.

One of the classic business models is that of Michael Porter, a Harvard professor of business. Professor Porter developed a "competitive forces model" which identifies five competitive forces in respect of an organisation.

- the threat of substitute products or services.

- the threat of the entry of new competitors;

- the intensity of competitive rivalry among existing firms in the market;

- the bargaining power of customers (buyers);

- the bargaining power of suppliers.

Any one of these elements, or their combination, may make a company take strategic action in the form of a change to their product or business operation.

It's not uncommon for a strategic decision process to involve the question "what business are we in?" This is not as crazy a question as it might appear, as markets, products, and the environment change increasingly quickly.

If you manufacture sportswear, because many people wear sportswear for general leisure purposes now, you could ask the question "are we a sportswear or a leisurewear company?" The answer could affect the type of sales outlet used.

If you manufacture and service a **consumer durable**, for example a washing machine, it might become **unviable** to manufacture the product in your own country because the product can be more cheaply manufactured overseas. Technological change may have made your company's process obsolete. The answer to the question "What business are we in?" may be: "the service business, not the manufacturing business". Following this decision, the company may have an opportunity to reorganise completely, and re-staff as a service company, with the reorganisation allowing for maximum streamlining and efficiency savings. What appears to be a crisis at first may be converted into an opportunity.

Respond to change
There are many changes which underpin business strategic decisions. Amongst the most significant are:

- **technology** affecting products or systems. The amazing thing is the speed – in the mid-70s an adding machine was the size of a printer. Within a generation the mobile phone has arrived and developed from a luxury item the size of a brick to an everyday essential which fits in a shirt pocket. The worldwide web is a phenomenon of the last twenty years.

- **social habits and fashion**. An example of this is the pub trade, which has completely changed in the UK. A generation ago people used pubs to drink in, and to have an occasional snack. Now the main part of pubs' business is providing food (and the food which is offered is much more up-market than in the past).

- **competitive activity.** The actions of a competitor may force the company into a strategic response, for example if the same product is offered at a reduced price.

- **innovation.** If, through a combination of design, research and development, marketing, and production, the company develops a new product, this may necessitate a company rethink as to its strategy (or even as to which business it is in).

- **changes in regulations.** Companies may decide to abandon methods of operation which are affected by new laws or which are now seen to contravene ethical standards (for example exploiting cheap overseas workers). There's more about ethics later. The way in which companies are directed and controlled from inside to ensure that they operate in a correct way, including conforming to regulations or ethical standards, is called "corporate governance".

Outsource

According to Wikipedia, outsourcing:

"Often refers to the process of subcontracting to a third-party".(13)

A company may outsource a function, such as product design or manufacturing, or an internal administration process, such as payroll.

The main **advantages** of outsourcing are:

- an outside company may have specialist skills which the company using the service doesn't have, or it may be able to provide the service more cheaply.

- the company reduces its permanent staff and fixed costs by outsourcing. (Permanent staff require national insurance payments to be made; also, normally a pension contribution, and can be difficult to fire.)

- the scale of the process may be more easily changed – in periods where the demand for the process is weak, for example, the process may be reduced more easily if provided by an outsourcing company than if performed "in-house".

The main **disadvantages** of outsourcing are:

- loss of control, for example of quality, but also of confidentiality of information or methods.

- the company providing the outsourcing service may go bankrupt without warning.

- when a company outsources, it loses part of itself and gains part of something else. As a result, the company culture may become "diluted".

Let's go back to the question of growth.

⑦ *How do companies grow?*

There are three main types of growth:

- **growth by merger or acquisition.** A **merger** is where two companies join together to form one new company, the original two companies ceasing to exist. An **acquisition** is where one company **acquires** (= purchases = **takes over**) another, by purchasing more than 50% of its shares.

    Arrangements where one company owns one or more other companies are called "**groups**". When group accounts are produced they are called "**consolidated accounts**". The company which owns another company is the "**parent**" company. It is not the head office – the head office is the headquarters inside the same company. The owned company is called a "**subsidiary**" company. Two companies with the same parent are called "**sister**" companies. Directors with responsibility for the group include "Group" in their title, for example Group Chief Executive Officer, or Group Financial Director. A company which owns another company but which does not itself produce anything is a "**holding company**".

- **vertical and horizontal integration.** Let's take the supply chain of a large supermarket. Simply stated, it looks like Figure 3.1.

115

Figure 3.1 A simple supermarket supply chain

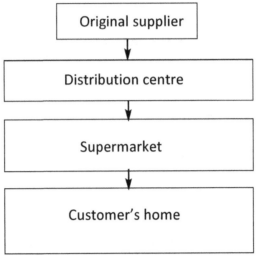

If a player is in the supermarket business and wishes to expand quickly, possibly to assume a more dominant position, they can expand in two directions: vertically or horizontally. Expanding horizontally would involve acquiring an operation at the same level in the supply chain, for example a large supermarket outlet buying further shops to increase its outlet strength and absorb excess distribution capacity. Expanding vertically would involve acquiring an organisation at an earlier or later stage of the supply chain, for example a supermarket outlet acquiring a supplier. The practice of expanding by acquisition, vertically up or down the supply chain, is called **"vertical integration"**. The practice of expanding by acquisition at the same level in the organisation is called **"horizontal integration"**.

- **organic growth.** This is where the same company expands due to increased output or sales.

? *What are the advantages of expanding by merger or acquisition?*

Companies find mergers or acquisitions attractive as a method of expansion because they provide the possibility of:

- **quick expansion of market.** Expanding by organic growth can be slow and uncertain to succeed.

- **securing new markets or selling new products** (diversification), thereby providing a spread of risk. Groups of companies where the constituent companies operate in different product areas are called "**conglomerates**". Alternatively, the new market may be for the same product but in a new geographical area. The opposite, which is organic growth, may be slow and not certain to succeed because of the response of competitors.

- **improved knowledge, and possibly systems**, from the newly acquired or merged company.

- **synergy** – the combined effect of two or more companies may be better than the sum of the individual parts.

- **getting rid of competition** in the form of the merged or required company.

Disadvantages of mergers and acquisitions

The disadvantage of a merger, as opposed to an acquisition, is that the original brand name can be either diluted (weakened) if the name remains in the new name, or is lost if the name is not used at all. (If the new name combines two existing well-known names, the new brand may however be stronger.)

In the mid-90s, two of the big five financial services organisations, Coopers and Lybrand and Price Waterhouse, merged. My experience, as a client of both, was of two quite different organisations, not least as Coopers and Lybrand seemed more American in style, and Price Waterhouse traditionally British. The new organisation, Price waterhouse Coopers, has a new brand image.

The disadvantages of growth by acquisition are:

- **expense** – often the acquired company costs more than its asset value. The profitability of the company being acquired can be used to value it, but its future profits after acquisition or as we say "post-acquisition" may not be assured if the brand name is lost.

- **loss of expertise** – often the directors and senior staff will leave the acquired company post-acquisition.

- **loss of control** – when a company acquires additional companies (or indeed is merged with another company) the question of control arises. Control may be difficult because the acquired company has methods of operation and systems which do not fit with those of the parent company. Instead of synergy there can be dysfunction, chaos, and inefficiency.

Case Study

In 2004 the UK supermarket Morrison's acquired Safeway and its 479 stores. A few weeks before the acquisition, Safeway changed its accounting systems, which led to Morrison's going back to manual systems and reporting poor financial results. (14)

There may not be enough managers left in the new company to control the larger business (especially if some of the key executives of the acquired business leave). Alternatively, the increased management may be difficult to organise. It can be very easy to underestimate the problem of not having sufficient management to effect and control the changes required post-acquisition.

- **brand failure** – It may be that the new, enlarged brand, representing the enlarged group, is not as attractive to customers as predicted, or as attractive as the previous small brand.

Risk

Risk is always present in company operations. It is particularly serious in the case of strategic decisions such as company acquisition. A key responsibility of the directors, which is part of their responsibility to provide corporate government, is to manage risk.

The main risks which companies face are:

- a bad event, resulting in adverse publicity.

- the loss of key staff following a bad event.

- taking incorrect action. For example, a company may buy another company without sufficient preparation and may not be able to manage the resultant organisation.

- not taking any action. Incorrect performance needs to be addressed and competitors will move quickly to overtake an inactive company. Also, companies thrive on development. Successful companies are always changing. Companies which take no action present no challenges and become stagnant and sterile.

- political risk, for example a change of regime or policy in a foreign country in which the company is operating.

- environmental risk – changes in the law, ecological awareness (for example anti- pollution legislation) and environmentally conscious behaviour (examples are the move away from clothes made from animal skins and the move towards organic and "Fairtrade" products).

- failure to manage liquidity, even if profitability is managed. This is a frequent cause of bankruptcy. (There is of course today the perceived risk present of depositing money with unsafe banks.)

- catastrophe – there is always the outside risk of natural disaster, accident, terrorist activity, or failure of complicated and sophisticated systems.

A classic example of a business hitting problems, for the perceived reason of insufficient action being taken in response to change, is the famous UK retailer Marks and Spencer at the end of the 1990s. In 1997 and 1998, the company made profits of over $1bn each year. Three years later they were below £150m. The share price fell by over two-thirds, affecting hundreds of thousands of small investors. The causes of the downturn? Analysed as being: Marks and Spencer were "considered to be a stodgy retailer"; margins and prices were held too high in the face of changing competitors who sourced product more quickly from low cost countries; no credit cards were accepted in the stores. Changes in top management and strategy have improved the company's profit levels since then, but net profit has still not climbed back to the level of 1998. (15)

Risk management

Risk management is a key element of business strategy. The most important responsibility in risk management is to minimise the possibility of the problem, which is the identified risk, occurring. Risk management involves predicting and assessing possible or probable external events which could or would negatively impact the business. In large companies this is a formalised procedure, driven by the directors, possibly involving a series of structured meetings and questionnaires, and also the senior management of the company. There additionally needs to be a discipline involved in decision making which involves asking awkward questions – the classic **"what if ...?"** questions. One of the most important functions of directors is to ask simple, but often awkward, questions.

Contingency planning is planning for dealing with a possible future development or event which, if it did happen, would or could cause serious problems. It is very important that there is a team of senior executives in place to develop and approve a contingency plan and who are prepared to take direct action should a crisis occur. Certainly one key action in crisis management is to communicate quickly and strongly to the important parties involved, and especially to the media.

Risk in general can be minimised by having the following in place in the organisation:

- a top level process to manage risk, including clear protocols for crisis management. This is a key part of the company's corporate governance;

- good people involved in risk management (who are capable of thinking "outside the box" and of asking appropriate questions);

- good managers in the organisation generally, and good, motivated, staff who will stick with the company through hard times;

- an effective communications strategy;

- a diversified product portfolio;

- enforced "**housekeeping**" procedures (in-house disciplines), especially in the area of protection of information (including the backup of computer files);

- strong cash reserves.

Making strategic decisions

How can a company approach making decisions of strategy?

If it's clear that something needs to be done, but it's not clear what, a good place to start is to analyse the present situation. (It is a business maxim that you cannot change direction if you don't know where you are.) It is also a good idea to start with basic fundamental questions, for example "what is our business about?" These discussions may involve reference to the company's basic documentation, for example, its Articles of Association, or the latest Mission Statement.

Companies often use a "SWOT Analysis" to plan strategy. (See the example in Figure 3.2). The "SWOT" looks at external and internal factors. Although it considers negatives (that is: Weaknesses and Threats), it is important to focus on the positives (Strengths and Opportunities). The strategic direction chosen may be an opportunity for a new start with a new team. It may be an opportunity to get some awkward decisions taken that otherwise might be avoided. And it may be a surprisingly uplifting process.

Figure 3.2 Example of SWOT analysis for stratgic decision-making

Strengths	Weaknesses
good product good people good reputation strong cash position	inappropriate cost structure technologically not developed products concentrated in one market
Opportunities	Threats
reduce cost invest in technology switch market	declining market strengthening competitors economic downturn

The problem with strategy

In business, as in life, it's relatively easy to make plans, and relatively difficult to make them happen (or, in business terminology, "**implement**" them). Managers and staff are usually completely occupied with the day to day running of the business. Implementation takes time, involves people doing things in a new way, may involve unpleasantness (often job losses), and may affect the morale of the people who are remaining, but affected by, the strategy.

Because of these potential difficulties some companies have their own planning function. The planning function not only devises the strategy but plans the practicalities of its implementation.

At a strategy meeting I once attended in Amsterdam, we, the directors, presented our 30 to 40 slides, outlining our strategy for the future. We sat back, waiting for the plaudits. Then, a small, bespectacled lady in a rather hesitant voice asked a simple question: "OK, but whose going to do all this?" This question was, I seem to remember, followed by an awkward silence.

The business world is also well populated with consultants. The right consultant can suggest solutions that would not otherwise be considered. They can effect the required change, and can generally can give the company a much needed makeover. However, consultants do come at a price – not only are consultants expensive, they take up time, can cause disruption, and, worst of all, can get it wrong!

The "people management" aspects of an organisation are, however, also absolutely key to formulating and implementing strategy, with or without the assistance of consultants. These are: well put together and well managed project teams; strong, empowered, management generally; good communications; and, of course, top level direction and support from the directors.

Business Ethics

Let's start with a few definitions:

 ## *What are ethics?*

"**Ethics**" is defined as: *"principles of right or wrong when applied to a person's behaviour or the conducting of an activity" (Oxford Dictionary of English).* "**Morals**", whilst being extremely close to ethics, does not have "or the conducting of an activity" in the same book's definition. So, if I see a person drop a £20 note, I might be morally obliged to tell the person and return the £20 to them. However, if I am a newspaper editor, I might feel it unethical to print a damaging story about somebody. According to Wikipedia, "**business ethics**" is *"the branch of ethics that examines questions of moral right and wrong arising in the context of business practice or theory".* (16)

 ## *How do we know if something is unethical in business?*

The question of whether something is intrinsically right or wrong can be unclear and subjective. If I favour a bright, strong, beautiful employee over somebody less attractive, and less intelligent, who is to say that I am wrong? I, and the person judging me, might believe in the concept of "survival of the fittest". In the film *Wall Street*, the character Gordon Gecko, played by Michael Douglas, makes the famous statement that "greed is good" because it is the basis on which the capitalist system, which creates wealth, works. The study of business ethics is not so much about whether something is right or wrong. It's about whether something is perceived to be right or wrong. Business behaviour can be considered to be right or wrong in two main ways:

- it can be considered against set "**norms**" (= usual or required standards). Experts call this a "**normative approach**".

- it can be perceived by society in general to be right or wrong. Experts call this a "**descriptive approach**".

An example of something that might be considered to be correct behaviour under the normative approach to ethics might be that of a lawyer who is not prepared to reveal the confidences of his client. The question of whether the lawyer actually is right or wrong not to do this may be a difficult one to resolve. Despite this, and even if the situation is not covered by the law, the lawyer is acting ethically because he is acting in accordance with the accepted code of his profession.

An example of something which might be considered unethical under the descriptive approach might be a senior public figure who is discovered having had a number of affairs. Most people in UK society would consider that behaviour to be incorrect.

Ethics therefore is not the same as the law. In fact, a law which is considered to have become unethical may finally be changed due to public pressure.

Two opposing viewpoints of business ethics

The extent to which businesses should attempt to be ethical, in addition to the requirements of the law, and should behave in accordance with the two approaches outlined above, has been the subject of a great deal of debate. There are two completely opposing viewpoints regarding business ethics:

- **Viewpoint One** stresses that a business (and therefore the directors) has a responsibility to act in a way which generates the maximum amount of profit for its owners, and which creates the best conditions for its stakeholders. A business should not concern itself with ethics according to this viewpoint.

- **Viewpoint Two** is that business not only has a responsibility to the shareholders but also to its consumers, who trust that the company is acting in an ethical way. The viewpoint is extended by saying that the company which is perceived not to be acting in an unethical way will find its profits plummet.

An example of consumer response to Viewpoint Two is the whole area of the treatment of animals. Many consumers now perceive that non-free range farming of animals and chickens is unethical and, as a result, sales of free range products have grown significantly in recent years.

Examples of the championing of ethical standards in production are the natural beauty products company The Body Shop and the Fairtrade movement.

Here are some further examples of practices which might be widely considered by the general public to be questionable or unethical (and which might be unethical according to the "descriptive" approach):

- using animals in experiments;

- genetically modifying crops;

- discriminating against women or old people;

- using disturbing pictures or images in advertising;

- sourcing product (coffee, bananas, cheap clothing) produced by low paid workers in third world countries;

- selling pornography, and selling goods harmful to health (is it right to sell high strength cider cheaper than water?);

- overfishing, deforestation, pollution;

- overstating profits and asset values to misrepresent the company's financial performance ("creative accounting").

How can a company manage its approach to ethical behaviour?

Companies are now managing their approach to ethics much more carefully than a generation, or even half a generation, ago. Back then it was largely a question of compliance with rules and regulations.

Business ethics forms part of the area of corporate governance. Corporate governance is, according to Wikipedia:

"The set of processes, customs, policies, laws, and institutions affecting the way a corporation (or company) is directed, administered or controlled". (17)

The people who are responsible for corporate governance in a company, and therefore for business ethics, are the people with overall responsibility for running the company: that is the directors. They exercise this responsibility on behalf of the shareholders, and possibly in response to shareholder pressure, and do this by developing, updating, and policing a code of ethical conduct.

Effective company direction also means that such an ethical code of conduct cascades down the organisation, and is understood and put into practice by the company executives.

In addition to the ethical standards of the company, corporate governance involves issues such as:

- the quality of internal control and internal audits.

- the quality and independence of external audits.

- the correct preparation of financial statements for external presentation.

- the suitability and strength of the board of directors.

- the management of risk.

- the long-term sustainability of the business in general.

One of the most dramatic business failures of all time was that of Enron, the US energy giant. After phenomenal growth in the fifteen years to the year 2000, Enron had an asset value of over $60 bn and 21,000 employees.

A questionable business practice employed by Enron related to their accounting policy. In essence this took the form of booking in the current year's accounts profits which related to future years' trading profits, which were connected to long-term contracts, and which were not guaranteed to happen. In addition, asset values were overstated and significant debt kept out of the books.

One deal, a 20-year entertainment supply contract with Blockbuster Video, involved Enron recognising (booking to their accounts) $100m of net profit even though the deal prompted questions about whether the agreed arrangement was technically feasible. In fact the whole thing failed, Blockbuster pulled out and the deal made a loss for Enron, but Enron still continued to recognise future profits.

The failure of Enron was clearly a failure of corporate governance, and therefore of the directors. Incorrect business practices were allowed and the company's finances were misrepresented. Following the resulting bankruptcy (Enron filed in late 2001) shareholders lost over $70bn, 4,000 employees lost their jobs and many executives were jailed.

The collapse highlighted the need, as part of a company's corporate governance machinery, for a much more tightly controlled external audit process performed by fully independent external auditors. Not only did Enron collapse but also, as a result, did their external auditors. This was one of the world's top five accounting firms, Arthur Andersen, who quickly collapsed with the loss of most of the 85,000 jobs. (18)

Part 4

The Success Recipe

Some Conclusions About Business Success

Let's try to bring all this together.

 So what does make a company a success?

First of all, good companies have a product or service which people want to buy. It needs to be a well designed, quality product, based on quality material, and produced or provided by a quality operation.

Successful companies tend to be **market driven**. They are focused on satisfying the exact segment of the market in which they are operating. This means that the other company functions point to, and contribute to, the marketing function – they do not operate in a vacuum. So, design and research and development must work to a marketing agenda. It is simply worthless to spend money and energy producing something which the market does not want. Not only should people want to buy the product but they should continue to want to buy it – the demand must be **sustainable**. The company must be able to identify change in the market and respond to change. Speed, in response to change, is absolutely vital.

Operations must deliver the product to the market – that means they must satisfy the requirements of the sales team – on time and at the right cost.

Excellent companies have strong financial managers who contribute to the commercial decisions, such as price setting, supply the required financial information to other company functions and provide the needed cash to keep the company going.

Excellent companies make delivering excellent service their top priority. They have efficient internal administration systems which make this possible. Also, in today's self-help environment, where customers order products or access account information online, they have simple, clear, user-friendly websites and procedures.

Successful companies have good corporate governance which ensures that they are well directed and avoid any bad (for example, unethical) practices. Good corporate governance in a company is key to sustainable profit.

Which all brings us to people. Good people and good quality go "hand in hand", even in today's sophisticated, impersonal, system-driven world. People are more important in an organisation than generally realised. Even in the armed forces, the police, or a government department, good people (and poor people) show through incredibly clearly. It's not just about pay and promotion prospects. People also respond to good values and good quality in an organisation, *but they especially respond to good bosses*. So recruiting and developing good managers, and potential managers, is key. People work for **people**, not mission statements or the brand image.

Well trained, motivated people deliver excellent service. They take authority, make decisions, try harder and go further to satisfy the customer. And by doing so they impress the customer with a with a sense of energy and enthusiasm which brings him back for more.

In order to achieve this, excellent companies have company-wide methods in place which aid people management – the right organisation management, the right philosophy of empowerment (of managers and their people), the right communications policy, and the right method of developing managers and staff. These things must be driven from the top of the organisation.

This then creates an energised culture where staff take action proactively. The task of the manager becomes to guide, and possibly to adjust ("**tweak**"), not to direct. When this happens, *the company develops maximum speed in response to change*. If staff have sufficient communication, if the right connections are made and if the right teams are formed between different activities and executives, the "virtuous circle" of proactive behaviour, energised culture, speed of response, and pace of development can be truly amazing.

How to get Noticed in an Organisation
(Ten Tips)

Tip 1

Have you ever met any really top people? I've met a few. I've spent evenings with the top people of top European companies. What I always reflect on, when I'm close to very senior people, is how very "ordinary" they are. Top people are not particularly big, tough, elegant, extrovert, or intelligent; nor are they normally workaholics. They normally don't do things in a particularly special way, have extraordinary skills, or have a charismatic glint in their eyes. I recently wined and dined a main board director of the international bank Santander at one of Portsmouth's top restaurants, only to find afterwards that he would have preferred to have gone to a fish and chip shop!

? *So what is it that senior people have, or do, that drives their success?*

The truth about top people is that they are normally ordinary people who have simply made a decision not to be ordinary. Not much of value in life happens without a decision first.

They have made a commitment to excel, and by excelling, to be a success. Based on this commitment, they normally do everything well, possibly a little bit better than other people.

So, Tip 1 is very simple:

Decide to be a success

"A man's worth is no greater than his ambitions." *Marcus Aurelius*

Tip 2

Having decided to be a success, you need to decide, success at what?

Who are you? What do you want to achieve? Status? Fame? Wealth? Or would you really, deep down, prefer to be a nurse or a social worker? What are you good at, or what might you become good at? What do you like doing? What do you believe in? The key word here is "you". You're unique. Don't blindly follow somebody else or try to be somebody else.

Be a bit selective: you need the right job, or the right type of job. It's difficult to be a success if you are a "square peg in a round hole". It's not a bad idea to write your own mission statement, or even a personal "SWOT", to help.

If you decide business is really for you, but you cannot decide on any specific area, choose the nearest fit, make a start and give it everything you've got. You can always change (or go round the world) later. Research it, and live the dream.

If you can decide, then you need to try to envision your life doing what you have decided to do successfully. Really imagine what success in your chosen area would be like.

So, Tip 2 is:

Define and envision success

"It is the chief point of happiness that a man is willing to be what he is." *Erasmus*

Tip 3

As you define and envision success, don't be afraid of aiming high – of becoming a director or partner of a large organization. It's not, in my experience, significantly more difficult to be at a senior level than at a junior level. It can in fact be smoother, in the same way that an aircraft, after taking off and climbing through clouds and turbulence, eventually hits "blue sky" and smoother flight.

It's certainly more stimulating and rewarding. Make "thinking big" a philosophy of life. (David Schwartz, in his book *The Magic of Thinking Big* recommends, for example, that if you go to a meeting, you should be a "front-seater", and not sit at the back for fear of being too conspicuous (19))

If you're going to be a senior business executive, try to achieve it early – say by forty. Business is demanding and it needs energy. A sobering thought that I've had, looking around me at times, was that the people who made it earlier than me were actually no better than me. They had, however, made a decision earlier and, as a result, made different choices, and done things differently.

Don't be afraid of communicating your ambitions to your boss. Don't crawl to senior people, but, as they say, don't "scratch around with turkeys" either. Take opportunities to talk to senior people but try to talk "away from yourself" and be well prepared.

If you're planning to start a business project, plan it on a big enough scale and ask for enough money. Really think it through and research it. Go to well qualified people for advice. Many businesses fail because the planning was not on a large enough scale and even more businesses fail due to lack of cash.

Tip 3 is:

Think big!

"Ah, but a man's reach should exceed his grasp. Or what's a heaven for?" *Robert Browning*

Tip 4

Don't be afraid. Dare yourself to be a success! The worst of the bad four letter words in the English language is:

Fear

Fear is public enemy number one – possibly the greatest killer of personal achievement. Fear is natural – heaven knows, I suffer from it. But, maybe you should ask yourself what you are afraid of? Making mistakes? Failure? Looking stupid? Failure and mistakes are, in fact, the best teachers in life.

> The great American inventor, Thomas Edison, was partially deaf, not considered to be good at schoolwork, had a flop with his first patented invention and had over a thousand failures in his attempt to invent the electric light bulb.

As for looking stupid, remember the key fact of life: people are not so interested in you (they're more interested in themselves). If they try to "put you down", smile and ignore it. What can they do to that? Putting down is a perverse form of respect. After all, as they say, "nobody kicks a dead dog". Countless times I've worried that I've looked stupid, only to find that I, alone, was aware of the situation. I recently got completely lost whilst giving a PowerPoint presentation to 45 MBA students in Latvia. On mentioning it later, I found that nobody had noticed and the class was considered to be a success.

Even if you do look stupid, well – its only pain. It's not going to kill you. As the philosopher Friedrich Nietzsche said: **"that which does not destroy me makes me stronger"**. You will get better by doing it wrong. A good way of overcoming fear is to think: what is the worse thing that is likely to happen? And, if it did happen, could I handle it? Normally, the thing does not happen, and almost always you could handle it!

Another good suggestion for handling fear is: live life a day at a time. It says in the Bible **"sufficient unto the day are the troubles thereof"** (*Matthew 6/34*).

> There is a story of a young batsman playing in his first top level cricket match. Just before going out to bat, he enquired as to how good the bowler was. "Well, let's put it this way", an older player said – "you won't see the first ball, and the second ball, if it doesn't knock you out, will probably knock out your middle stump". The batsman's knees started to shake. He started to stagger out of the pavilion. Then the older player smiled and added: "but there's one thing you should remember, lad: good as he is, he can only send them down one ball at a time."

It really is one of the best things about the future: it comes to us a day at a time.

The best way of overcoming fear, a day at a time, is to take action. This might mean speaking to somebody, researching on the internet (it's never been easier to get information), or trying something. You will find that when you take action your fear melts away like the mist in Scotland.

So, here's Tip 4:

Overcome fear with action

"Every man , through fear, mugs his aspirations a dozen times a day"
Brendan Frazer

Tip 5

The truth is that business is a bit of a game. One of the rules of the game is that it's not generally enough to do things well. You have to do things well and also you have to give the impression of success.

Impression is (almost) everything in business. Financial markets and share prices go up and down because of impression. There is never much time in business and people, especially senior people, make judgements quickly. It's a very quick tilt between being perceived as a winner and being perceived if not as a loser then as not one of the winners. You cannot help yourself more than by working at your presentation.

Choose a manager you respect and try to emulate (copy) him. See how many of the points mentioned in the "People Management" section he puts into action. Impressions tend to be formed in "clusters". If a senior person sees two or three good qualities, like intersecting lines, in an individual, then he will form a good impression of that individual.

So, in addition to providing the right information, put a shine on your shoes, and a crease in your trousers. It's not necessary to "power dress", or be unduly formal, but it is necessary to be appropriately dressed. One of my colleagues, a CEO, was criticised, then not taken seriously, because he liked to wear a Mickey Mouse tie. The higher you go, the more important is appearance. When did you last see a British Prime Minister wearing a brown suit or an Hawaiian shirt?

I'm not suggesting that success is all "smoke and mirrors". Appearance however, when added to good performance, can be very powerful. Written reports or PowerPoint presentations are also part of personal presentation.

These things are not easy, and need work and practice. Here are a couple of pointers:

- Don't assume knowledge on the part of the listener or reader (do you know the old business maxim: never ASSUME, because when you assume you make an "**ASS** of **U** and **ME**"). Other people will not understand the detail as you do. Think about what the information will mean to them. Avoid technical jargon, and give the complete report or presentation a title, and each point or visual a clear heading.

- **avoid detail.** Senior people hate complexity when trying to receive information. It takes much longer to write something on one page than on five pages. Take the detail out of the main part and put it at the end (of a report) or on a handout (if a presentation). Try to get to the main point, don't get stuck on the micro. **Nothing identifies mediocrity in a person as clearly as overconcentration on the micro.** Stick it on your fridge!

  Americans talk about **"KISS" – Keep it Simple, Stupid!** Keep written information Simple.

  Don't write: "Efficiency figures are down 3.8778 % or 3.6329 depending on whether or not we include..."
  Do write: "Efficiency is down by just under 4%. This is because... and means that...."

Below is a piece of nonsense. Can you express it in three words? See the next page.

People of advanced age, predominantly of the male gender, have, in most but not all cases, a pronounced tendency to lose their faculties of recollection. This, whilst not categorically proven, is empirically observable, and appears to be a robust working hypothesis.

Old
men
forget
(**Shakespeare, Henry V**)

Which do you think is the more beautiful? Or powerful?

- **if you are giving a presentation:** do everything slowly, especially at the start. **Don't start with the detail.** Start by talking about your audience ("thank you for coming ...") even before you introduce yourself. The first minute is very important – practise it. Finish with a clear finishing formula ("thank you for your attention. That concludes my presentation".) This works much better than "are there any questions?" You will get a round of applause after the first, and a silence after the second.

- in an interview situation: if you are late (in the UK), of course call before-hand and apologise, but don't rush into the interview. Go to the men's room and smarten up. Pull your socks up (literally!) Slow down. The first minute is essential. Make sure your hands are dry, give your interviewer a firm handshake, look him in the eye and, if possible, use his name. If he's with an older colleague, be sure to address the older colleague by name at some point in the interview. It will be worth five questions answered correctly. Sit to the back of the chair and – **smile!**

Tip 5 is:

Take care over presentation

"It is only shallow people who do not judge by appearances. The true mystery of the world is the visible, not the invisible." *Oscar Wilde*

Tip 6

> When I took up my first management role in London, my direct manager appeared to be very little affected by whether I did good or bad work. In fact, sometimes he seemed to be more pleasant when I made a mistake. For several months this was a mystery to me and did little for my motivation. The reason finally hit me: what I was doing was of relatively little importance to him. What was important to him was HIM and what HIS manager was doing to him.

It's extremely important in business to think through the mind of the other person.

When I started asking myself what my boss's boss was doing to my boss, and **why** my boss wanted things from me, our relationship seemed to improve. As stated above, a key lesson in life, which most people don't learn, is that people are interested not in you, but in themselves. If somebody is boring you at a party, the quickest way to get rid of them is to start talking about yourself. So, even if people ask you about yourself, the way to get people to like you, is to talk about them – their problems and their tasks. Nowhere is this true more than in business. Whether you think you are good or not so good, don't talk about it. Talk to others, especially good people, about what **they** are doing. You will learn and you will become popular and respected.

It works in an interview as well. I was once videoed being interviewed. What I saw horrified me: every sentence I uttered seemed to contain "I" or "me":

I, I, I , I, I, I, I, I, me, me, me, me, me, me, me, ...

Try instead to connect what you can do to what you've read that the interviewer is doing, or to what you understand that his organisation needs. It will make you stand out, and here's the thing: even if you get it wrong, you will get marks for trying.

This idea can be extended: successful executives don't think about their job inwardly, in a vacuum. They think about what they can contribute outwards.

Good people think in terms of their customer. Everyone has a customer in an organisation: it may be the person who uses your service or it may be the person who uses your financial information. Try to satisfy their requirements, ask them what they need (be selective and don't overdo it).

A great example of this concerns financial reports. Many executives have a fear of finance and accountants. The wrong approach is to spend an enormous amount of time and energy perfecting the report by yourself, then push it out to your customers with lots of technical jargon. The right approach is to find out what they need to know and how they would like it presented, to present it as simply as possible, and in a way that is as well connected as possible to the customer's problem. I once agreed with a top engineer at Gillette, who had a problem understanding financial variances, that we should mark positive variances with a ☺ and negatives with a ☹ – he really was a lot more interested after that.

If you can tailor your report to your customer it is more likely to be "pulled" into correct shape by, or in the right direction, by him and others. In general, in the business world, it is better to be pulled up than to try to push yourself up.

A final thing: don't resist your boss when he recommends a change to your report. If you do what he recommends, he will own it and champion it, and pull it where it needs to go.

Tip 6 is:

Think outwards

"Ask not what your country can do for you. Ask what you can do for your country." *J F Kennedy*

Tip 7

One of the few things I remember from my MBA course is a professor of production management saying: "if you remember only one thing from your MBA course, remember The 80/20 Rule. It does work!"

The **80/20 Rule** (Pareto's law) states that:

"For many events, roughly 80% of the effects come from 20% of the causes".

What this means is that, in many given samples, roughly 20% of the value will come from 80% of the volume. This is true, for example of collecting money. If 100 customers owe you £1,000,000 together, don't try to collect from all 100 immediately. Analyse them, select the top 20 customers, and try to collect £800,000 from them.

This does not only work for financial things. If you have 10 problems and solve 2, often the other 8 then appear trivial. It's also probably true that, of all the people you know in an organisation, 20% will have 80% of the influence over your progress and destiny. Think out who they are, what they need, and how to access them – with information, or by contributing to their agenda. Try to get yourself "pulled up" by them, rather than trying to "push" yourself up blindly.

What this means in practice is that it's essential to spend time planning how to do important things, and making what you do important. Today we live in a world where people are compulsively busy. Food must be eaten whilst working and walking down the street must be done whilst texting or shouting into a mobile phone. *Take a break* – it is possible – and spend time planning what really needs to be done. Many people in business are busy fools. They don't get much of importance done. Remember Peter Drucker: Be effective as well as efficient.

Get to the main point of what you are trying to do or say. A good way to do this is to ask the question: *"What does that mean?"* until you are ready. To take a simple example:

"Efficiency figures are down"

"What does that mean?"

"So, costs are up"

"What does that mean?"

"So, cash is down"

"What does that mean?"

"So: we need to make some savings. I suggest ... or ...

A final thing: don't be a perfectionist. Normally being successful is not about doing things perfectly. One of England's most famous pre-war entertainers, George Formby, was reported as saying that he never thought he was that good – he just seemed to have what people wanted. If you do things perfectly you will run out of time. What seems perfect to you will not seem perfect to your boss. You can spend 80% of the time you spend on a complete task perfecting the task. Instead, achieve the essence of what you are trying to do, present it well, and let it go. It will get knocked into shape by other people, and will probably be better and better received as a result.

So Tip 7 is:

Work the big issues.

"Action expresses priorities." *Mohandas Ghandi*

Tip 8

When I talked about managers, I mentioned good organisation. This is important for everybody in life, as well as in business. Normally the most useful thing I do in a day is to plan the next day!

I'll be brief here but let me just mention three small things that work for me:

- **keep your desk tidy.** Only have on your desk the things relating to the task in hand. Remove used cups, tissues, and pens that don't work. That way you won't spend time looking again and again at the same irrelevant things, you won't get distracted, and you will impress the right people (the wrong people will say you are not busy).

- **be punctual.** It's difficult. Get everything you need ready well before you need to leave the house or the office. Interrupt a boring task in order to do this. You'll feel better about the task, and you'll feel better about what you're leaving to do. Get to where you are going early – you can always make a call or use a laptop from the car park or the departure lounge.

- **do a long boring task by the clock.** It sounds wrong but it does work. Intersperse mental tasks with physical ones. Work at, for example, writing up some meeting minutes until exactly 3pm, then do a task which involves

143

more action (if you're at home, do the washing up, make a phone call or prepare what you need to leave the house. You'll end up working longer and feeling better).

- **If you're having difficulty starting a task, divide the task into two parts**: first, think about it and get everything ready (papers information etc), but don't do it. Later, simply and mechanically, start the task. The preparation will be easier because you are not going to do the task, and starting the task will be easier because you are well prepared.

It really is a crime how much energy is wasted, and how many otherwise good people fail, because of poor organisation.

So Tip 8 is:

Get organised!

"The secret of all victory lies in the organisation of the non-obvious."
Marcus Aurelius

Tip 9

I said earlier that business is a bit of a game. It's not a Greek tragedy or a penance. Peter Drucker, in his great little book *The Effective Executive, emphasises the importance of getting the right person into the right job.* (20) So, don't suffer a bad situation or a bad boss for too long. It will eat you up and your ship will start to sink. Discuss the situation amicably and, if necessary, move. It is much easier to move early in your career than later.

Bob Hope, the famous American comic, when asked at the age of 99 how he kept so young looking, replied simply: "Oh – you gotta keep moving."

Don't get stuck in a rut. Take action.

Tip 9 therefore is

Keep moving.

"You are responsible for your life. You can't keep blaming somebody else for your dysfunction. Life is really about moving on." *Oprah Winfrey*

Tip 10
Robert F. Kennedy (brother of John F.) said:
"Don't get mad, get even".

Don't try to get things done by making an impatient gesture. Don't complain about people. Don't criticise or blame, moan, or try to "shaft" people. Nobody is interested in your moods and problems. Be judged and respected on how much it takes to make you angry. Senior people don't often get angry. In my experience, the way to get things done is not to make a big gesture but to nudge the problem forward, pleasantly and persistently. People like pleasant people. Pleasant people become popular people. And popular people get promoted. Follow President Johnson's advice (he's the one that came after Kennedy) which is to be an "old shoe/old hat" type of person. Be comfortable to be with. Be positive and friendly. The world loves an optimist.
My final tip, Tip 10 is:

Be nice!

"He gains everyone's approval who mixes the pleasant with the useful."
Horace

So, all that remains for me to say is:

Thanks for reading, and good luck!

References

1 Page 13:
Non-profit organizations. (2010). Retrieved March 24, 2010, from the Wikipedia website: http://en.wikipedia.org/wiki/Non-profit_organizations_

2 Page 18:
Public limited company (2010). Retrieved March 24, 2010, from the Wikipedia website: http://en.wikipedia.org/wiki/Plc_(UK)

3 Page 26:
Sandra Dawson is interviewed as part of Market Leader Business Briefings (2000) video, unit 3. Harlow, England: Pearson Education

4 Page 29:
Peter f. Drucker quotes. Retrieved March 24, 2010, from the ThinkExist.com website: http://thinkexist.com/quotes/peter_f._drucker/_

5 Page 30
Drucker, Peter F.(1970) *The Effective Executive*. London: Pan, p.1

6 Page 44:
Kotler, Philip (1999). *Kotler on marketing: how to create,win, and dominate markets / Philip Kotler*. New York; The Free Press, p.37

7 Page 46:

Kotler, Philip (1999). *Kotler on marketing: how to create,win, and dominate mar-kets / Philip Kotler*. New York; The Free Press, p.20

8 Page 46:

Innovation (2010). Retrieved March 27, 2010, from the Wikipedia website: http://en.wikipedia.org/wiki/Innovation

9 Page 102:

Continuous Improvement Process (2010). Retrieved March 24, 2010, from the Wikipedia website:
http://en.wikipedia.org/wiki/Continuous_Improvement_Process

10 Page 103:

Schaefer,P.(2006) *The Seven Pitfalls of Business Failure*. Retrieved March 24, 2010 from http://www.businessknowhow.com/startup/business-failure.htm

11 Page 103:

Greene,G.(1971). *Travels with my Aunt*. London: Penguin Books,p.43

12 Page 109:

Business Definition for: Strategy (2010). Retrieved March 25, 2010 from the BNET Business Dictionary website: http://dictionary.bnet.com/definition/strategy.htm

13 Page 114:

Outsourcing(2010). Retrieved March 24, 2010, from the Wikipedia website: http://en.wikipedia.org/wiki/Outsourcing

14 Page 118:

This information is included in the Wikipedia website:
Morrisons (2010.) Retrieved March 24, 2010, from the Wikipedia website: http://en.wikipedia.org/wiki/Morrisons

15 Page 120:

This information is included in the Wikipedia website:
Marks and Spencer (2010.) Retrieved March 24, 2010, from the Wikipedia website: http://en.wikipedia.org/wiki/Marks_&_Spencer

16 Page 125:
Business Ethics (2007). Retrieved March 24, 2010, from the Wikipedia website: http://en.wikipedia.org/wiki/business_ethics

17 Page 128:
Corporate Governance (2007). Retrieved March 24, 2010, from the Wikipedia website: http://en.wikipedia.org/wiki/Corporate_governance

18 Page 129:
This information is included in the Wikipedia website:
Enron Scandal (2010). Retrieved March 24, 2010, from the Wikipedia website: http://en.wikipedia.org/wiki/Enron_scandal

19 Page 135:
Schwartz, David J.(1959). *The Magic of Thinking Big*. Englewood Cliffs, N.J.: Prentice Hall, p. 64

20 Page 144:
Drucker, Peter F.(1970) *The Effective Executive*. London: Pan, ch. 4

A-Z of Key Terms

New Titles by Legend Business